T0246591

HAUNTED PUGET SOUND

IRA WESLEY KITMACHER

Haunted
America

Published by Haunted America
A Division of The History Press
Charleston, SC
www.historypress.com

Front cover: *A View, Far North of Seattle, Down the Deception Pass, Separating Whidbey Island (Left) and Fildago Island (Right) to Tiny Deception Island. Courtesy of Library of Congress; Carol M. Highsmith, photographer.*

Opposite: Puget Sound, Washington. *By Ken 1843 via Pixabay.*

First published 2024

Manufactured in the United States

ISBN 9781467157841

Library of Congress Control Number: 2024937578

Notice: The information in this book is true and complete to the best of our knowledge. It is offered without guarantee on the part of the author or The History Press. The author and The History Press disclaim all liability in connection with the use of this book.

I dedicate this book to my beloved family.
—Ira Wesley Kitmacher

CONTENTS

Introduction 7

    Why I Wrote This Book 7

    My Beliefs and Approach 12

    Investigating and Fact-Finding 16

PART I. DEFINITIONS

1. Folklore, Customs, Superstitions and Urban Legends
    Underlying Hauntings 20

2. Ghosts 26

3. We Don't Know a Millionth of One Percent About Anything 32

PART II. A HAUNTED JOURNEY AROUND PUGET SOUND

4. Puget Sound 36

5. Olympia 41

6. Communities Near Olympia 51

7. Tacoma 55

8. Communities Near Tacoma 65

9. Seattle 69

10. Communities Near Seattle 80

11. Everett and Surrounding Area.......................................86

12. Port Gamble, Whidbey Island and Other Towns.............91

13. Bellingham and Surrounding Area.................................98

14. Port Townsend and Port Angeles 102

15. Native Legends 109

Conclusion...115

Bibliography...119

About the Author...125

INTRODUCTION

WHY I WROTE THIS BOOK

From the beginning of time, people have told stories and tales about mysterious and scary experiences, events and a life beyond this physical one. One of the first ghost stories was about the biblical King Saul, who conjured the ghost of the prophet Samuel through the Witch of Endor. These stories were often a mix of truth, exaggeration, fear, humor and wishful thinking. The more interesting of them took on a life of their own, became legends and were passed from one generation to the next. The stories in this book are not mine but rather tales I discovered, researched and am chronicling that have been passed down by word of mouth and other means for decades, if not centuries. Hopefully, I am shedding new light, garnering fresh insights and offering unique interpretations of these tales. I can't, in some cases, corroborate the accuracy of these stories, but nonetheless believe they round out the fascinating history of Puget Sound.

Sometimes the stories in this book (and other folkloric tales) continued in their original form, and other times, they were embellished or altered. These stories have been told by European pioneers and settlers, Natives, homegrown citizens and people from every corner of the globe. As a resident of Washington and the Puget Sound region in particular, I'm fascinated by its history, folklore, ghost stories and explanations for the otherwise unexplainable. This is the third book I have written and had published that

Painting of Saul and the Witch of Endor, 1828. *Courtesy of Smithsonian, William Sidney Mount, artist.*

ties in with this genre (I briefly describe the prior two in the following pages). In addition to this book of Puget Sound ghost stories, the other substantive area of "dark stories" told in the Pacific Northwest (Oregon and Washington specifically) is about cryptids ("imaginary creatures"), curses and folklore. I address those stories in my upcoming (October 2024) book *Pacific Northwest Legends and Lore*.

In my first published book, *Haunted Graveyard of the Pacific* (2021), I focused on hauntings at the mouth of the Columbia River, where the river meets the Pacific Ocean, as well as the coastal areas between Portland, Oregon, and Seattle, Washington. Some believe the term *Graveyard of the Pacific* applies to only the confluence of the Pacific Ocean and the Columbia River. In fact, the graveyard stretches along the Pacific Northwest coast—from Tillamook Bay in Oregon past the treacherous Columbia Bar (the world's most dangerous entrance to a commercial waterway) near Astoria, Oregon, then up the Washington coast, the Juan de Fuca Strait separating Canada from the United States and on up the western coast of Vancouver Island. Furthermore, the graveyard includes the waterways and the coasts that hug those waters. Over two thousand ships and countless lives have been lost to the Graveyard of the Pacific. That book proved successful: it was named a "recommended read" by several magazines, and my publisher (The History Press) adapted it into a children's book, *The Ghostly Tales of the Pacific Northwest*.

In my second published book on Oregon and Washington ghost stories, *Spirits Along the Columbia River* (2022), I focused on the second-largest river after the Mississippi by volume in the United States, which unites all parts of the Pacific Northwest. Historically, the river garnered much interest on the part of explorers from Spain, Great Britain and the United States. These countries struggled over possession of the river as they sought the legendary but imaginary Northwest Passage (across the North American continent; a route was discovered in the early twentieth century across the Arctic). Their hope, unfulfilled, was to find a route by water to the Pacific Ocean from the Mississippi River. This is what led to President Thomas Jefferson commissioning Lewis and Clark's 1805–06 Corps of Discovery expedition. This competition between nations, as well as the settling of the region, led to much pathos, conflict, opportunity and achievement. Frontiersmen, adventurers, soldiers, boatmen, early settlers, Natives and others suffered tragedies and death, resulting in numerous haunted tales.

In this, my third published book on area history and folklore, I focus on Washington's Puget Sound area, which is an inlet of the Pacific Ocean and interconnected waterways and basins connected to the Pacific and the coastal areas that bound them. It extends from the city of Olympia in the south to the colorfully named Deception Pass in the northern part of the Sound, with the cities of Tacoma, Seattle, Everett, Bellingham and others in between. Puget Sound is the second-largest estuary (a partially enclosed coastal body of mixed salt water and fresh water, or brackish water) in the United States, after Chesapeake Bay in Maryland and Virginia. I serve as an onboard historian and speaker on cruise ships sailing on Puget Sound (and other American waterways) and have led both nautical tours of Puget Sound on an old-fashioned schooner and land-based history and haunted folklore tours of Washington's capital, Olympia.

Puget Sound got its name from British explorer George Vancouver, best known for his 1791–95 expedition, which explored and charted North America's northwestern Pacific coast regions (including what would become Alaska, British Columbia, Hawaii, Oregon and Washington) onboard his ship the HMS *Discovery*. He named Puget Sound in 1792 in honor of his Huguenot (French Protestant) lieutenant Peter Puget. Coastal

Pacific Northwest Native totem pole. *By LonaE via Pixabay.*

Salish Natives, who preceded Vancouver, called it Whulge, meaning "sea, salt water, ocean or sound."

Washington was one of the last parts of the United States to be explored and settled, making it seem more "wild," in the "old days" and today, to those who visit and live here than other parts of the country that were settled earlier. There is no better way to discover the beauty and history of this area than to explore its cities, towns and waterways and their history and folklore (including haunted tales). It is known for great hiking, boating, camping, fishing, biking, clamming, golfing, cranberry cultivation, oyster farming and tourism, while state parks with nineteenth-century military forts and national historic sites welcome history enthusiasts. Bald eagles, black bears, elk, deer and other wildlife call the area home. While Washington offers breathtaking, idyllic scenery, it has also been identified as one of the most haunted states in America. The spirits of frontiersmen, adventurers, boatmen and early settlers seem to cling to the cities and towns. Other lingering spirits are said to include those of Natives whose lands were stolen and burial grounds desecrated, kidnapped or "shanghaied" sailors, soldiers, murderers and murder victims. The dramatic events and, at times, trauma people experienced in life seem to leave an energy that is permanently etched and embedded into the land and waters, resulting in many of the ghost stories we'll discuss.

Chilling tales of paranormal phenomena abound in this northwestern corner of the United States, and it's no wonder the vampire and werewolf *Twilight* books (and movies), the pirate treasure movie *The Goonies*, the TV series *Supernatural* (one of my favorites), the remake of *The Fog* and the drama-mystery *Twin Peaks* were made or based in Oregon, Washington and nearby. Even the movie *The Shining*—for which Oregon's Timberline Lodge served as the Colorado-based Stanley Hotel in exterior shots—includes a can of Willapoint Minced Clams, sourced in the Graveyard of the Pacific at Willapa Bay, Washington.

The Puget Sound region is steeped in history and folkloric tales. From possessed parks to creepy underground tunnels to hotels with spirits as permanent guests, there are many haunted attractions to visit. Some areas, including Seattle, have high concentrations of haunted houses, ghost tours and scary sightings. Other ghosts seem to prefer more rural places. Some ghosts go much further back. Natives have lived in the area for at least ten thousand years, according to archaeological records, and some of that Puget Sound history is downright eerie. Sightings of ghostly Natives regularly occur at haunted burial grounds across the state as well as at old forts. There seem to be many ways to get your haunted chills in the Evergreen State (Washington's nickname).

The dark skies, wind and fog that frequent the Puget Sound region round out the atmosphere of mystery and dread, coupled with fires, earthquakes, tsunamis, volcanoes and other natural and man-made disasters. So, if you see someone on land who appears out of place or hear ghostly words on the wind, check again—it might be the forlorn spirit of a lost soul reaching out.

My second published book (unrelated to the Pacific Northwest) was *Monsters and Miracles: Horror, Heroes and the Holocaust* (2022). That book was centered on a very different world: it takes place primarily in the Nazi-occupied Europe of World War II. In that book, I wrote about my father, Al Kitmacher, a Holocaust survivor who led his family to temporary safety and, through miracles, survived the Warsaw Ghetto and five Nazi death camps, and my mother, Pearl Harris, a World War II U.S. Navy veteran, who through her military service helped those suffering at the hands of the Nazis. I interwove their stories with World War II and Holocaust history. This included the Nazis' and their victims' underlying folklore (the Nazis believed they were descended from werewolves and their enemies were vampires); horror, hero and superhero stories (who knew Captain America, Superman and others were created to persuade Americans to enter the war against the Nazis?); and beliefs in monsters, angels and the supernatural. I am working with a European tour company on an eleven-day tour of Poland and Germany based on that book, which I will colead.

MY BELIEFS AND APPROACH

Those who believe in ghosts and paranormal phenomena say restless spirits haunt Washington, pointing to the tales of Natives, early settlers and others. Though I would not describe myself as a full believer in these stories, I find them fascinating and would like to believe that some of these legends, or at least parts of them, are based in fact and are true. Furthermore, having lost both of my parents, relatives, friends and pets, I firmly hope there is a better place beyond this life. I think that, in part, fuels my interest in stories of "life after death."

There are several reasons I'm fascinated by U.S. history, mysterious folklore and ghost stories. I was born and grew up in Massachusetts, one of the first and most important areas in America to be settled by European immigrants. Massachusetts is full of history, including Plymouth Rock, where the Pilgrims disembarked from the *Mayflower* in 1620, and America's first Thanksgiving, where colonists and Natives celebrated their thanks for a bountiful harvest in 1621. The Bay State (one of its nicknames) played a key leadership role in the Revolutionary War and independence from Great Britain and is where great patriots like John Adams and Paul Revere were born. I take pride in these historical events. Massachusetts was also home to one of the more

Settlers' wagon. *By Momentmal via Pixabay.*

mysterious and dark periods of American history, which fascinates me: the Salem Witch Trials of 1692 and 1693. That was the ultimate example of humans' preoccupation with and fear of the supernatural and the unknown causing them to act in unfathomable ways toward their neighbors. I also lived in the Washington, D.C. area, greatly appreciating the history, the museums and the role government plays in our everyday lives. In fact, my pride in being an American led me to spend my career working for the federal government. I've traveled extensively through and explored historic areas, including Gettysburg, Pennsylvania, and Williamsburg, Virginia. These experiences have deepened my love of history and the mysterious folklore that accompanies it. I've also lived in the Southwest and the western United States, learning the importance of the "Old West," ghost towns and nautical history. Many Americans, during the nineteenth century, believed in "manifest destiny," an almost divine right to expand the country from the original thirteen colonies to encompass the territory stretching from the

Atlantic to the Pacific Ocean (many times, unfortunately, at the expense of Natives). Each part of the United States has a fascinating history and accompanying mysterious and scary tales to tell.

My background is an eclectic one that—while on the surface it might not appear to be tied directly to the subjects I write about—prepared me for this work. I retired from the U.S. government in 2019 after thirty-six years as a senior executive and manager and in other roles in the western United States and Washington, D.C. I am also a consultant, legal expert witness and licensed attorney (California). From the early 1980s to the mid-2000s, while based in the San Francisco Bay area, I made numerous trips throughout the Pacific Northwest to teach government leadership courses. It was during that time that I became fascinated by the region's atmosphere and history.

My wife, Wendy, and I moved from the West to Washington, D.C., for my work. My last role was that of chief human capital officer (human resources director) for a federal agency. I was named that agency's senior executive of the year in 2019. After living in the D.C. area for thirteen years, we retired and decided to move back west. Our focus quickly centered on the Pacific Northwest. Our reasoning was based on the climate, history and beauty of the area. On retiring, I quickly found I had no desire to fully retire; I had to do something more, something worthwhile that would reflect my desire to acclimate to my new home and make a positive impact. To paraphrase American statesman Benjamin Franklin: if one wishes to be remembered, they should either write something worth reading or do something worth writing about. I chose the former!

I have also served as a college and university professor teaching graduate and undergraduate courses at Georgetown University in Washington, D.C.; Portland State University in Oregon; Grays Harbor College in Aberdeen, Washington; Clatsop Community College in Astoria, Oregon; and Western Nevada College in Fallon. I developed a program on the haunted history and folklore of Oregon and Washington that I taught at Clatsop Community College. I have been featured on TV shows and radio programs, in documentaries and newspapers and at museums, bookstores and conferences where I've spoken about the history and haunted folklore of the Pacific Northwest. I designed and led haunted and history trolley tours of Washington's Long Beach Peninsula along the Graveyard of the Pacific. I am a commissioner on a county historic commission in Washington and a member of the Historical Writers' Association.

I have traveled extensively within the United States and spent time in Europe, Canada and Mexico. Whenever I have a chance, while traveling,

I participate in ghost tours and other activities that focus on an area's history and haunted folklore. I have done this in the United States in places like Charleston, South Carolina; Gettysburg, Pennsylvania; New Orleans, Louisiana; Salem, Massachusetts; San Francisco, California; Seattle, Washington; Sleepy Hollow, New York; Tombstone, Arizona; and Williamsburg, Virginia. In Canada, I have visited Halifax, Montreal, Toronto, Victoria and Vancouver. In Europe, I have traveled through Austria, Belgium, France, Italy, Germany, Greece, Hungary, the Netherlands, Poland, Switzerland and the United Kingdom. In Mexico, I have traveled to Ensenada and Tijuana.

Growing up, my favorite books to read and movies to watch were those about the "classic monsters," including Dracula, Frankenstein, the Creature from the Black Lagoon, the "Headless Horseman" of Sleepy Hollow, the Wolfman and others. I have a particular affinity for two movies by Abbott and Costello (my favorite comedy team): 1946's *The Time of Their Lives* (involving Revolutionary War ghosts!) and 1948's *Abbott and Costello Meet Frankenstein* (in which they face off against many of the classic monsters). I enjoy reading about "inexplicable" and paranormal events (a person instantaneously combusting!) and books like *Ripley's Believe it or Not* and *Chariots of the Gods* about the weird and mysterious. As an undergraduate, my favorite courses were about Greek and Roman mythology and classic ghost stories (although my major was human resources management). Maybe these interests were a precursor to writing books like this one.

I have written this book in the form of a road map, starting in the south and working our way north, exploring the Puget Sound area, including the waterways and nearby land-based areas, and intertwining long-standing ghost stories, folklore and history. I view my role as multifaceted: historian, investigator, interested tale-teller, prideful resident and tour guide. It is through these lenses that I wrote this book. As humans, we have particularly short memories; few remember tragedies that happened decades, let alone a century, ago. Other than the *Titanic* and a few notable others, we have virtually no memory of long-ago shipwrecks and other disasters that resulted in multiple deaths. These disasters were all too common in the days before satellite navigation, GPS, cell phones and other safety measures. One of my primary reasons for writing books like this is to try to help preserve historical stories that might be lost over time.

INVESTIGATING AND FACT-FINDING

Using an evidence-based, investigatory approach to research and analyze reported supernatural phenomena, I found a wealth of information on the region's haunted history in Native oral history, settler and adventurer accounts and books, newspapers from the mid-1800s to the present day, recorded stories, government records and social media. I have not included legends or stories that lack evidence, and I have taken great pains to include, in the bibliography, all the source materials I reviewed—and that informed my writing—making sure to give credit where credit is due.

It is my nature to question whether these tales are based on fact and logic. I pride myself on my careful research, which I have practiced over the last forty years while wearing many different professional hats. But in researching these tales, it became clear to me that not everything can be proven beyond a reasonable doubt.

In conducting investigations and fact-finding, there are different types of evidence to be reviewed and methods to collect them, including the following:

- Real evidence consists of those items that played a role in the story or legend, including evidence that can be touched, smelled, seen or in some other way sensed.
- Documentary evidence, which documents the events in question, includes government reports, newspaper accounts, university studies, logs and others.
- Demonstrative evidence includes animations, drawings, diagrams and maps.
- Testimonial evidence consists of witness statements, interviews with those who observed or experienced the events and oral history.
- Digital evidence emanates from media and technology including movies, documentaries, social media, blogs, emails, telephone calls and others.
- Site visits to the locations, buildings and physical sources of the legend or story are very helpful.

In a book like this, there are bound to be overlaps and similarities between legends. This is in part because tales tend to emanate from similar circumstances (haunted houses, theaters, cemeteries, lighthouses, etc.) with similar evidence (cold spots, disembodied voices and footsteps, brushing

Delving into research. *By DariuszSamkowski via Pixabay.*

of hands, apparitions, etc.). I am sensitive to readers finding repetitive information and have tried to include examples that are unique.

Finally, I chose the stories to discuss based on five factors:

1. The length of time a tale has been told—or how old it is.
2. How widely spread (frequency and/or prevalence) the telling of the story appears to be.
3. A story's impact on the surrounding community.
4. The sources for and amount of proof or evidence of the story that exists.
5. The interest stories have generated and may elicit.

PART I
DEFINITIONS

CHAPTER 1
FOLKLORE, CUSTOMS, SUPERSTITIONS AND URBAN LEGENDS UNDERLYING HAUNTINGS

Puget Sound has its fair share of folkloric tales related to hauntings and other supernatural topics. *Folklore* literally means the lore of the folk, or people. *Lore* means knowledge, so a fair definition of *folklore* would be "folk knowledge." When I say *knowledge*, I mean the accepted, conventional wisdom of a society that is taken for granted as being true. Folklore includes traditional knowledge and beliefs that are passed on from generation to generation. Folklore or lore has a rich history, and all legends have an origin story. In many cases, tales were created by rural, frequently poor peasants and others, who expressed a shared identity by way of traditional stories.

Folklore takes many forms, including material (art, architecture, textiles), music, narrative (legends, fairy tales) and verbal (jokes and proverbs). Englishman William Thoms coined the word *folklore* in 1846 and used it to replace the terms *popular antiquities* and *popular literature*. It differs from history, which is made up of past events and changes in society. It is thought that folklore gives us the wisdom to understand history from a different point of view. Folklore showcases humankind's problems and successes. While much of folklore plays a positive role in a society's culture (enhancing a sense of history and commonality), some folklore (e.g., the German Nazis' belief in their superiority) has a very negative impact.

Folklore includes imaginative tales that cover a wide range of topics: romantic encounters, origins of popular holidays and lighthearted fables. Lighthearted American fables include those of Paul Bunyan (the giant

An antique explorer's map. *By Darkman Art via Pixabay.*

woodsman who, with his blue ox, Babe, created major landmarks—including Mount Hood in Oregon); John Henry, the famed railroad builder; Johnny Appleseed, the scatterer of apple seeds; and Davy Crockett, the pioneer who fought and died for Texas's independence from Mexico at the Alamo. In this book, instead of those lighthearted fables, I examine the darker side of folklore made up of ghost stories. Many believe these stories are based on truth; I do my best to explore that.

Stories of hauntings serve many purposes. For believers, these tales may simply document paranormal activity. For others, they may help explain that which is not easily explained. For others still, such tales can be a fun escape from reality—like the experience of telling ghost stories around a fire. Whatever the reason people tell ghost stories, these tales are a fascinating part of an area's history and reflect local, regional and broader anxieties and fears. Moreover, ghost stories are often at least partially based on underlying facts—sometimes those facts have been spun into urban legends with the passage of time and the evolution of tales with each retelling. Maybe the stories are simply true from the start—you be the judge!

Haunted folklore has been part of human culture since the first century AD, when Roman author and statesman Pliny the Younger described the specter of an elderly man with a long beard and rattling chains who haunted a house in Athens, Greece. Other examples of haunted folklore include the story of the ghost of Anne Boleyn, who was the second wife of

The Alamo. *By 12019 via Pixabay.*

British King Henry VIII and executed in 1536 for witchcraft and treason; sightings of her spirit have been reported in the Tower of London, where she was imprisoned and put to death, and in her childhood home, Hever Castle. The ghost of Thomas Jefferson's vice president, Aaron Burr, who famously dueled and killed founding father Alexander Hamilton, has been reported roaming the streets of the West Village in New York City. Benjamin Franklin's ghost has been seen near the American Philosophical Society Library in Philadelphia, Pennsylvania. Many people have reported seeing ghostly soldiers still fighting the July 1–3, 1863 Battle of Gettysburg on the battlefield of the same name (experts say that battle changed the course of the American Civil War in the Union's favor). The World War I battlefields of Gallipoli (Turkey) and the Somme (France) are also sites of numerous ghost sightings. British Prime Minister Winston Churchill reported seeing the spirit of the United States' sixteenth president, Abraham Lincoln (my personal hero), in 1944 at the White House. Churchill stepped out of the bath and reportedly said, "Good evening, Mr. President. You seem to have me at a disadvantage."

In my research, I have found there to be connections between haunted folklore and history, societal events, politics and other cultural touchstones occurring at about the same time. One example of this is the Salem witch trials of 1692 and 1693 in Massachusetts. The history is clear: nineteen people were tried and found guilty of witchcraft (in service to the Devil) and executed. The Puritans, who founded Salem, were firm believers in the supernatural. The societal and political connections include a gender bias against women (who were the majority of the accused), a desire to "keep women in their place" and racial discrimination, as well as economic battles between the haves and have-nots. Women had no legal identity as individuals. Some men believed women were more emotional than men and had difficulty controlling their behavior. Women tended to resent this repression, and there was tension. Legal records were kept by men, legal proceedings were led by men and judges and juries were made up of men. The result was that more women than men were accused of being witches (over two hundred) and executed (thirteen of twenty by hanging; a man—eighty-year-old Giles Corey—was pressed to death with stones). Three additional women died in prison, after being accused of witchcraft. Society used repressive authority, in part due to religious anxiety. Additional historical elements included race and color. (Tituba, one of the first to be accused, was a South American, dark-skinned, Indigenous Indian enslaved woman.) Furthermore, there was friction between the rich and the poor; those with money and land (in this case, primarily the Porter family) and those without (mainly the Putnams), who battled for power; and the young (the accusers) and the old (the accused). These age-old societal battles were fought by some using the Devil and witchcraft as proxies for the more real-world problems at play. Finally, some Salem residents at the time held the supernatural and paranormal belief that the Devil was possessing "afflicted" female victims. Since the Salem trials and executions, there have been many reports of the spirits of those executed. Some of the most haunted locations include the Joshua Ward House (once owned by malicious sheriff George Corwin, who tortured victims and was cursed by Giles Corey), the Witch House (once owned by Judge Jonathan Corwin, who sentenced victims to death) and the Old Burying Point Cemetery.

In my experience, some history purists bristle at the retelling of these folkloric tales. They dispute the topics and events as not history and therefore of little or no value. I disagree. Although folklore is not regarded as history by some, to many—including in the academic community—folklore is seen as an integral part of a region's history. Folklore is studied at Harvard, the University of California at Berkeley and other leading universities and is considered an important way to understand different cultures. Further, folklore—especially haunted tales—draws people's interest in a way that straight history too often does not. In this book, I intertwine folklore with history, and though I try to be clear about which is which, I believe the two go hand in hand.

I distinguish folklore from customs that relate to behaviors and practices, not knowledge or belief, though they overlap in that people generally behave in a way that is in line with their society's beliefs. The United States has many customs those in the rest of the world find strange. These include presidential turkey pardons ahead of Thanksgiving; holidays such as Groundhog Day in Pennsylvania, where a groundhog predicts the weather; cherry pit spitting in Michigan; roadkill cook-offs in West Virginia; the National Hollerin' Contest in North Carolina; pumpkin chucking in Delaware; continued use of the imperial system of measurement (e.g., inches, feet, pounds, gallons, etc.), whereas much of the rest of the world uses the metric system; using a primarily single-colored currency with similar-looking bills, whereas much of the rest of the world uses far more colorful money; supersizing fast food; requesting condiments (ketchup, mustard, salt, etc.) with meals; requesting "doggie" or to-go bags for unfinished restaurant food; using a lot of ice in our drinks (in many other countries, that's seen as "watering down" drinks); giving a thumbs-up (in fact, in some countries, it's seen as rude, like sticking up one's middle finger); a separate sales tax (in most other countries, this is already reflected in the item's price); referring to the United States as "America" (it's considered politically incorrect in Central America, Mexico, South America and other parts of the world to refer to the United States in that way); writing the date as month, day, year (most of the rest of the world uses day, month, year); opening gifts in front of the gift giver (you may be seen as greedy for doing so); requiring personal space with no physical contact; tipping at restaurants; chatting with strangers (in many other countries, people aren't as comfortable with this); laughing out loud (in some Asian countries, it's considered rude to show your teeth); expecting free refills of soft drinks and coffee; going into debt for a college degree; trick-or-treat practices (some countries don't see this as primarily for children); sitting in the back seat of a taxi (in some countries, this comes across as elitist); and staying optimistic, no matter the situation (seen as a particularly American trait).

Superstitions are like folklore in that they are often passed from one generation to the next and have their basis in stories dating back hundreds if not thousands of years. However (and there is overlap), unlike folklore—which may or may not be true—superstition is more likely based on inaccurate assumptions, irrational fears, misunderstandings of science, obsessive-compulsive tendencies (uncontrollable, reoccurring thoughts, obsessions and behaviors) or other tricks of the mind. Superstitions can include fear of walking under ladders, stepping on a crack in the sidewalk or breaking a mirror, out of fear that something bad will come of it. Again, although many superstitions appear to be absurd on their face, sometimes they can become reality. "Never say never" is a good motto to use.

A subcategory of folklore is urban legends, contemporary folktales typically described as having happened to a family member or friend (not to the person telling the story—presumably to keep the teller out of a negative light or to protect the teller's reputation), with cautions about moral behavior. They tend to be relatively recent (not centuries old) and are often spread verbally by word of mouth, newspapers, e-mail and social media. An example is the story of poisoned Halloween candy or candy with razor blades placed in it by strangers to harm random children. These stories have been reported for about fifty years but appear to be generally false and alarmist, with very few people ever having been harmed in that way.

The definition of *legend* is a story from the past that is believed by many people but cannot be—and/or has not yet been—proven to be true.

CHAPTER 2

GHOSTS

The word *ghost* comes from Old English and refers to the human spirit or soul of the deceased, separate from the individual's physical body, which can appear to the living. Other names for ghosts include *haunt*, *phantom*, *specter*, *spirit*, *shadow*, *apparition*, *presence* and *vision*. The Latin word for ghost is *exspiravit*, with different categories of ghosts classified as *agmine exspiravit* (ghost train), *navis exspiravit* (ghost ship) and so forth. It is thought these spirits have not passed on; rather they are trapped or connected to earthly memories, the living or unfinished business. Often, the deceased met with sudden, unexpected death, whether through an accident or violent, tragic means. Another form of ghosts, graveyard spirits, are thought to haunt the locations where their physical bodies were buried after death. Though different cultures have different theories about ghosts, most have some belief in an afterlife.

Attempted communication with the dead via séances and other means (necromancy) has been part of civilization since at least the time of biblical King Saul. In the ancient Roman Empire, the Lemuria festival called for food offerings to the dead. Mexico's Day of the Dead, in which dead ancestors are celebrated, is descended from the sixteenth-century Aztec custom of celebrating ancestors with an All-Souls' Day. Sir Arthur Conan Doyle, author and creator of the great detective Sherlock Holmes (who first appeared in the 1887 novel *A Study in Scarlet*) said (proclaiming his belief in the supernatural—I'm paraphrasing) that at no time in history have humans not found traces of paranormal interference, but they have frequently been late in recognizing it.

Spiritualism and necromancy (attempting to communicate with the dead) became popular during the Victorian era of the mid- to late nineteenth and early twentieth centuries (during the reign of the United Kingdom's Queen Victoria, 1837–1901). Between four and eleven million in the United States alone identified themselves as spiritualists. It was not just a U.S. phenomenon, as spirituality was a very popular topic around the world. Some practitioners of necromancy were dishonest hucksters who tried to cheat believers. However, the belief in ghosts was strong, and such historic luminaries as writer and humorist Mark Twain, abolitionist and orator Frederick Douglass and Queen Victoria attended séances. It is thought part of the reason for the rise of spiritualism was the high rate of childhood mortality in the mid-nineteenth century (between 20 and 40 percent of children died before the age of five). President Abraham Lincoln's wife, Mary Todd Lincoln, visited Georgetown's mediums after losing three of her four children. Interest in spiritualism was also heightened due to the three-quarters of a million soldiers who died in the U.S. Civil War (1861–65). It spiked again after World War I (1914–18). Another contributing factor was the rise of photography, which was said to capture ghosts in images (although many such photos were proven to be manipulated). There were strong opponents of spiritualism, including organized religion and magician Harry Houdini, who made it his goal to debunk as many spiritualists as possible.

Ghosts are said to generally take one of six forms:

ECTOPLASM OR ECTO-MIST: A vaporous cloud, floating above the ground, that appears white, gray or black (although, in the 1989 movie *Ghostbusters II*, it appears as green slime). Reportedly witnessed in graveyards, on battlefields and at historical sites, among other places.

FUNNEL OF LIGHT: Experienced in homes or historical buildings, along with cold spots: a wisp or a swirling funnel, spiral or vortex of light. Many of us have experienced cold spots and wondered if it's an air circulation issue or perhaps something of a paranormal nature.

INANIMATE OBJECT: Ghost ships, trains and other vehicles believed to be controlled by the undead who died in accidents or wrecks or suffered sudden and unexpected ends. Examples include: the old City of Albany ghost train, featured in *Ghostbusters II* (really an amalgam of multiple train wrecks), said to have killed over one hundred people when it derailed in

1920, and the *Flying Dutchman*, a legendary ghost ship said to be doomed to sail forever, most likely based on seventeenth-century Dutch East India Company ships.

INTERACTIVE PERSONALITY: The spirit of a known deceased person, family member or historical figure. The spirit is said to be able to make itself visible, speak or otherwise let someone know it is present. It may be visiting to comfort the living or perhaps because it believes the living want to see it. I provided an example earlier of British Prime Minister Churchill reportedly seeing the spirit of President Lincoln.

ORB: A transparent or translucent hovering ball of light. Sometimes orbs go unnoticed but are captured in a photo or video. I have witnessed these (I'll describe them in the following pages), although the question of whether they are paranormal events or undulating dust particles lingers. These entities are often seen in television ghost-hunter programs.

POLTERGEIST: Poltergeists—German for "noisy ghost"—are thought to be able to move or knock things over, make noise, manipulate the physical environment, turn lights on and off, slam doors and start fires. They are often depicted as dangerous, as in the 1982 Steven Spielberg horror movie *Poltergeist*.

There are other forms ghosts and the undead are said to take. Doppelgangers appear to be people who look like us (who hasn't had someone say, "You look just like so-and-so!") and are said to be spirits and harbingers of our impending demise. Legend has it that if you meet or see your doppelganger or "spirit double," you will die. Similarly, if someone refers to seeing or meeting your "evil twin," it is said something bad is going to happen to you. Doppelgangers share some similarities with the Wraith, which we'll talk about in the following pages.

Ghouls are another form of the undead: legendary evil, demonic beings that inhabit burial grounds and other deserted places, rob graves and feed on corpses. It is said a ghoul is created on the death of a man or woman who savored the taste of human flesh (a cannibal). Ghouls not only eat the dead but can also prey on the unwary living. They can paralyze their victims with a touch. (Elves are immune to this!) Author Edgar Allan Poe described ghouls as not man, woman or human. They are thought to assume disguises, ride on dogs and hares and lure travelers off main roads by setting fires at night.

Like legends about ghosts attaching themselves to places (battlefields, cemeteries, hospitals, houses, others) to take care of unfinished business, remain near loved ones or seek revenge, there are legends of spirits attaching themselves to dolls, furniture and other belongings that were important to them in life. Haunted dolls and belongings that are possessed by ghosts (or evil spirits) are familiar storylines in some scary movies and television programs. The story is that these items, possessed by malevolent spirits or demons, become living objects that torment and/or kill the humans around them.

Dolls, by their nature, both inspire love and give some people a terrible feeling. Dolls look like babies or miniature people, with motionless bodies and glassy, lifeless eyes. It's easy to assign personalities to dolls, puppets and human figurines. Possibly the most infamous and haunted doll is named Robert. Key West, Florida painter and author Robert Eugene Otto owned the doll beginning in 1906, and it is now housed in the Fort East Martello Museum. Lore has it Robert was jinxed by a Bahamian practitioner of voodoo (a custom in the Caribbean and the southern United States combining Roman Catholic elements with African magic, including sorcery and possession of spirits). The doll is said to have spoken to children, laughed maniacally, run from room to room, knocked down furniture and launched murderous attacks against its owners.

Other supposedly haunted belongings include dybbuk boxes, said to contain the spirits of the dead that would terrorize the living if released; asylum doorknobs, literally taken from old asylums for the mentally ill and reputed to have the spirits of those unfortunate patients imprinted on them; djinn (or genie, a mythical being resembling a human but with magical powers) masks infused with supernatural powers; shoes and clothing to which the dead hang on; and paintings and photographs that have somehow "captured" the image of the dead.

The woman in white, the weeping woman or La Llorona are similar stories found in the Americas and around the world. Generally, they follow the same story or scenario: a woman who was married to an unfaithful man takes her own life and sometimes the lives of her children. She then becomes a vengeful spirit, exacting her revenge on unfaithful

Old doll. *By Desertrose7 via Pixabay.*

29

men. She may appear to these men as a damsel in distress, asking for their help, only to kill them soon after.

I've had my own experiences with what I would describe as, seemingly, the supernatural, in which it could be argued ghosts or unseen forces played a role. In one, my father- and mother-in-law (with whom I was close) died within twenty-four hours of each other in 2020. My wife and her siblings stayed with their parents during their last days, providing comfort. My wife told me that one day, she entered the room where her mother had died and saw a coin sitting in the middle of the carpet. She picked it up and saw it was a German pfennig from the 1870s. No one knew where the coin came from, and neither of my in-laws collected foreign coins. Knowing I collect antique coins, my wife brought the pfennig home to me. I placed the coin on the bookcase behind my desk while I was writing my first published book, *Haunted Graveyard of the Pacific*. At one point, I got up to go to the restroom, and when I returned to my desk, I found the coin sitting in the dead center (pardon the pun!) of my office chair. That seemed odd, and I tried to re-create how the coin could have gotten there but was unable to. I placed it on the bookcase behind my desk, worked for a few more hours, then again got up and left the room. On returning, I found the coin had moved again,

After the Battle of Gettysburg, 1863. *Courtesy of Smithsonian, Alexander Gardner, photographer.*

this time to my mouse pad. I again tried to re-create how this could have happened, including seeing if the coin would stick to my hand, but could not. I then said a little prayer to my mother-in-law, telling her I would take care of her coin. It hasn't moved on its own again. Interestingly, coins have been tied to death since ancient Greece, where it was believed coins (placed over the deceased's eyes) were needed to pay Charon the ferryman for transportation to the underworld. Some believe finding a coin after a loved one's death means they're watching over you.

In a second event, I was touring the Gettysburg, Pennsylvania battlefield, and while driving, I saw a very authentic-looking Civil War reenactor—tattered clothing, covered in soot or dirt—in full uniform (not uncommon). I glanced back at the road, then again at the reenactor—but he was gone. There were no trees or buildings behind which he could have gone. Was I seeing things? Soon after, I heard a story of an incident said to have occurred during the making of the 1993 movie *Gettysburg* (the only movie ever filmed on the battlefield and one of my favorites). Actors reenacting the battle were running low on blanks (a firearm cartridge without a projectile that resembles and sounds like a real weapon). The movie crew asked anyone with extra blanks to come forward, and a man in a very authentic-looking uniform came forward and offered cartridges. When the crew attempted to use them, they found they were in fact real and later dated them to the Battle of Gettysburg. No one saw the reenactor again—was he a ghost?

On a separate tour of Gettysburg, I was on a ghost tour using ghost-sensing equipment, including dowsing rods (a tool, dating to ancient Greece, used to find objects, including bodies of water underground and said to have supernatural qualities, although skeptics say unconscious muscle movements in the hands cause the rods to move). While I was holding the rods, one in each hand, they seemingly pivoted on their own, the end of each touching my shoulders. I asked the tour guide what had happened, and she said, "That's your mother hugging you." I hadn't told the guide that my mother died just a few weeks before.

Finally, on a tour of the Astoria, Oregon haunted underground, I videotaped (using my smartphone) and played back images of ghostly orbs hovering and independently changing direction, making right-angle and other turns. Skeptics may say they were dust particles, but they appeared to me to be on their own power.

CHAPTER 3

WE DON'T KNOW A MILLIONTH
OF ONE PERCENT ABOUT ANYTHING

I t is easier to dismiss claims of hauntings and other supernatural
phenomena than to prove their existence. In most cases, there simply is
no rock-solid proof of these reported paranormal occurrences. However,
I'm frequently reminded of famed inventor Thomas Edison's statement
about not knowing a millionth of one percent about anything. I fully believe
what Edison said is true. The world around us may contain additional
elements and/or information that we simply don't appreciate or understand.

Thomas
Edison, 1907.
*Courtesy of
Smithsonian, Pach
Brothers Studio.*

Please join me as we journey along and explore the breathtaking Puget Sound area of Washington in search of ghosts, haunted folklore, supernatural phenomena and other mysterious things that go bump in the night. I hope you enjoy reading this book as much as I enjoyed writing it. I strongly encourage you to explore the area and visit (of course, following all applicable rules and laws and respecting privacy, hours of operation, etc.) the many businesses and landmarks open to the public that we'll discuss.

PART II
A Haunted Journey
Around Puget Sound

CHAPTER 4

PUGET SOUND

Puget Sound is an incredibly scenic part of the United States, with deep waters, colossal mountains, thick rainforests and varied wildlife. I'm fortunate: my home office, where I wrote this book, overlooks the waters of Puget Sound in Olympia, Washington (the state's capital). Puget Sound is defined as the region of marine waterways and basins consisting of brackish water (fresh water from rivers and lakes, mixed with salt water from the Pacific Ocean) that is a portion of the Salish Sea, a part of the Pacific Ocean located in Canada's British Columbia and Washington State. The Salish Sea is a larger system of inland marine waters that includes the Straits of Georgia and Juan de Fuca. Puget Sound is about 100 miles in length, from Olympia in the south to Admiralty Inlet (the waters separating Canada and the United States) in the north. Although Chesapeake Bay is a bigger estuary, about 200 miles long, Puget Sound has a substantially larger amount or volume of water. By comparison, the San Francisco Bay is about 60 miles long. The coastline around Puget Sound measures 1,332 miles long, and it's estimated it would take eighteen days to walk the whole shoreline—if it were passable and legal to enter all adjacent lands!

The Puget Sound region was created when microcontinents collided and attached themselves to the North American continent about fifty to one hundred million years ago. About fifteen thousand years ago, the region was covered by part of the Cordilleran ice sheet. About ten thousand years ago, glaciers carved deep and complex troughs, creating what we know today as Puget Sound. Fresh water from river basins flowing from

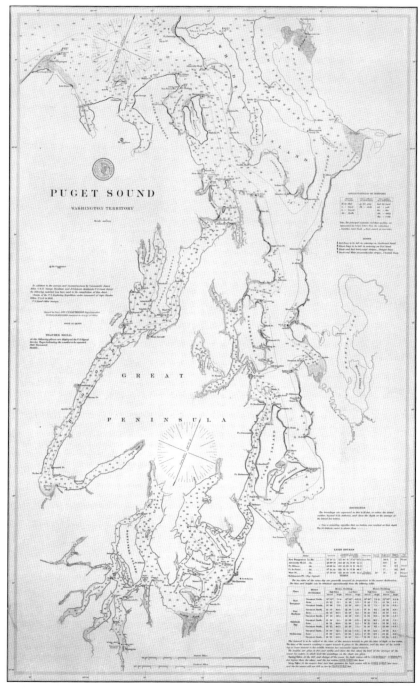

Map of Puget Sound, Washington Territory, 1889. *Courtesy of Library of Congress, U.S. Coast Guard.*

the Olympic and Cascade mountains through glacier-carved channels and branches mixes with salt water from the Pacific, filling the wetlands, marshes and bays of Puget Sound.

Natives first settled in the Pacific Northwest at least ten thousand years ago. They migrated from Asia south though what is today Alaska and Canada. The land and waters, including Puget Sound, provided rich natural resources for Natives: wood (Natives excelled in wood carving, including totem poles), salmon and other fish, oysters and other shellfish, deer and other mammals, herbs and birds. The Spanish were the first Europeans to arrive to the area, in 1774 (just prior to the American Revolution). The British soon followed. The Natives at first had cooperative relationships with many of these European powers. This would change when the Pacific Northwest became part of the United States.

British explorer George Vancouver, in addition to naming Puget Sound in 1792 for his second lieutenant, Peter Puget—who explored the main channel—later had Vancouver, British Columbia, and Vancouver Island (both in Canada) as well as Vancouver, Washington, named for him. Great Britain had sent Vancouver to the area in 1790 to help resolve the Nootka Sound controversy, a dispute between the British and the Spanish over rights to the territory. Vancouver died at the age of forty in 1798, most likely from malaria he contracted while exploring the West Indies in the 1770s.

In 1846, the British (who ruled over Canada and part of the Pacific Northwest) and the United States agreed on a new border at its present location, referred to as the forty-ninth parallel (stretching from Canada's British Columbia to Manitoba and from Washington to Minnesota in the United States). Many Native people woke up living in a wholly different country, under different laws; tribes were displaced. Until 1846, relationships with Natives were stable as the United Kingdom's Hudson's Bay Company developed ties based on trade and furs. As Americans—or Bostons, as they were sometimes called—arrived and claimed lands and resources under the 1862 Homestead Act, relationships changed. Natives became frustrated with U.S. land policies that rewarded squatters and encouraged immigration. In 1854, Native chief Leschi negotiated the Treaty of Medicine Creek, protecting some Native lands. However, in 1855, gold was discovered in eastern Washington, and U.S. miners crossed Native lands. Several miners were killed, and Washington territorial governor Isaac Stevens declared martial law. Natives were placed on reservations, and wars took place between the United States and Natives, including the Puget Sound War of 1855 and 1856 (with an undetermined

Technical Report 2007-04

Beaches and Bluffs of Puget Sound

Prepared in support of the Puget Sound Nearshore Partnership

Jim Johannessen and Andrea MacLennan,
Coastal Geologic Services, Inc.

Beaches and Bluffs of Puget Sound publication, 2007. *Courtesy of Library of Congress, U.S. Government.*

number killed on both sides). Chief Leschi was subsequently caught by U.S. troops and hanged in 1858. His ghost has been repeatedly seen where he was hanged in the town of Steilacoom, which I'll discuss a little later. In 2004, Chief Leschi was posthumously exonerated by Washington State, which recognized him and the other Natives as legal combatants.

Puget Sound is critical to Washington's economy, culture and environment. The Puget Sound region holds about two-thirds of the state's population. Puget Sound's remarkable water circulation supports its thriving ecosystem. Port Jefferson (named in honor of President Thomas Jefferson, who sent Lewis and Clark to explore the region), about five miles northwest of Seattle, is the sound's deepest part, with depths up to 930 feet. Its average depth is about 450 feet. Sea life in Puget Sound includes dolphins, giant Pacific octopus (weighing up to 150 pounds with an arm span of up to 20 feet—it is thought the legendary kraken is based on this creature), gray whales, humpback whales, orca or killer whales, porpoise, sea lions and sea otters, as well as clams, mussels, anemones, sea stars and crabs. The sixgill shark, sixteen to twenty feet long, is found in Puget Sound but is a rare sight and not dangerous to humans. The only two recorded shark attacks in Washington State were by great whites in Grays Harbor, to the southwest, near the Pacific Ocean. There are twenty fish species found in the sound, including cod, herring, rockfish, salmon and sturgeon.

Puget Sound has many excellent deep-water harbors, including Seattle, Tacoma, Everett, Port Angeles and others. The naval shipyard at Bremerton adds military shipping to the sound's large volume of ship traffic and trade. The Inside Passage (also called Marine Highway) between Alaska and Washington ends in Bellingham to the south. There is regular ferry service to and from Bellingham to Alaska. (My family and I rode the ferry from Bellingham to Ketchikan in southern Alaska in September 2023; it was spectacular.)

While Native peoples have been in the area for more than ten thousand years, members of the Simmons-Bush party, in 1845, were the first U.S. citizens to settle in the Puget Sound region, founding New Market (which later became Tumwater).

The Puget Sound region, like the rest of the Pacific Northwest, is rich in history and haunted folklore. These tales have been passed down through settler accounts, government records and Native oral history. We'll start our haunted tour at the southernmost point on Puget Sound, Olympia, and travel north and westward.

CHAPTER 5

OLYMPIA

Olympia is the capital of Washington and the county seat and largest city of Thurston County (with the county's population over three hundred thousand people). It is sixty miles southwest of the state's biggest city, Seattle, and is a cultural center of the southern Puget Sound region. It regularly makes "best place to live in the U.S." lists and has been described as a cool (behavior-, clothing- and customs-wise) and laid-back waterfront city (sitting at the southernmost end of Puget Sound). My wife, Wendy, and I live in Olympia, and I designed and lead nautical history and haunted tours on the waters of Puget Sound and a similar walking tour of Olympia's historic downtown. I tell many of the stories you'll read in this book on my tours. Olympia's is a story of earthquakes, fires, storms, conflict with Natives, shipwrecks, anti-Chinese sentiment, the Oregon Trail, murder and violent crime, the Dead Zone (also called, in many cities, the Tenderloin—so named in 1876 by a New York City police captain who said he could afford tenderloin steak with the bribes he received there) and the red-light district. It is also a story of rebirth, growth and perseverance.

In 1846, some fifty years after George Vancouver explored the area, Edmund Sylvester and Levi Lathrop Smith (the town's initial name was Smithfield) jointly claimed the land that is now downtown Olympia. In fact, the first reported White settler's death in Puget Sound was that of cofounder Smith, who, in 1848, on his way to an Oregon Territorial Legislature meeting, experienced an epileptic seizure, fell out of his rowboat and drowned.

Bird's-eye view of Olympia, Washington Territory, 1879. *Courtesy of Library of Congress, E.S. Glover and A.L. Bancroft & Company.*

In 1850, the town took the name Olympia because of its excellent view of the Olympic Mountains to the northwest. The Customs District of Puget Sound for the Washington Territory was established in 1851 by the U.S. Congress; Olympia was made the site of the federal customshouse and was the only recognized American town and port of entry on Puget Sound. It also offered the closest access to the waters of Puget Sound for those traveling by land from Portland, Oregon, and the Columbia River. In November 1851, the schooner *Exact* disembarked with passengers at Alki Point, which was the beginning point of the city of Seattle. In February 1852, three settlers—Arthur A. Denny, C.D. Boren and William N. Bell— sailed to the south toward Olympia and found the water deep enough to form a port; they staked land claims along the water. Given its status as a port of entry (through which goods were shipped), Olympia was made the capital of the new Washington Territory (broken off from the initial Oregon Territory) in 1853. The Treaty of Medicine Creek was initiated with local Natives in 1854, which U.S. officials interpreted as requiring the Natives to cede their prime farming and living space. One of the Native leaders, Chief Leschi, was outraged and refused to give up Natives' ownership of this land. He and his people fought for the right to own their territory, sparking the Puget Sound War in 1855. The war ended with Chief Leschi's execution; he was hanged in 1858—and his ghost has been seen repeatedly where he was hanged in the nearby Washington town of Steilacoom.

Olympia's population steadily expanded as immigrants traveling the Oregon Trail settled there. When Olympia was first settled by Americans, the main way to access the town was by boat, as roads were mostly impassable. The lower Budd Inlet (the primary portion of the Sound bordering Olympia) was a mudflat. Given extreme low tides, larger ships had to land at the wharf and unload their contents onto small steamers that could maneuver through the shallow waters. This continued until the mile-long "long wharf" was built in the late nineteenth century. The area was served by a fleet of hundreds of steamboats known as the Mosquito Fleet. On January 28, 1859, Olympia was incorporated as a town, and in 1882, it became a city. From 1896 to 2003, Olympia Brewing Company (located in nearby Tumwater) brewed Olympia Beer (using Olympia artesian water flowing naturally to the surface); its slogan was "It's the Water." Puget Sound waters outside of Olympia were dredged of dirt and mud (creating a deeper waterway) in 1911 and 1912, and twenty-two new blocks were added to the downtown using the soil. In 1925, the first marine shipping docks were completed. Fires damaged Olympia's downtown in 1870 and 1882. The 1949 Olympia earthquake (7.1 on the Richter scale) killed eight and damaged many historic downtown buildings, many of which were demolished. Parts of the city also suffered

Olympia, Washington, 1903. *Courtesy of Library of Congress, Edward Lange.*

damage from earthquakes in 1965 (6.5) and 2001 (6.8). Interstate 5 was built, passing through Olympia, in the 1950s. Percival Landing (Olympia's primary port), dating to 1877, has been rebuilt several times, was remodeled in 2011 and now holds public spaces for meetings, the arts, public mooring and festivals. Olympia had a population of 55,605 at the time of the 2020 census, making it the state's twenty-third-largest city.

The nineteenth-century Oregon Trail stretched approximately two thousand miles west from Missouri toward the Rocky Mountains and ended in Oregon's Willamette Valley. The northernmost spur of the trail ended in Olympia's Sylvester Park (marked by a brass plaque placed on a boulder in the northwestern corner of the park in 1913 by the Sacagawea Chapter of the Daughters of the American Revolution). The trail was the primary land route for those wishing to travel west, with three hundred to four hundred thousand immigrants traversing it between 1840 and 1860. They came looking for inexpensive, fertile land and gold and for greater opportunities. However, the trail was dangerous; about thirty thousand lives—10 percent—were lost. Tremendous hardship and death were too-frequent occurrences for travelers along the trail. It is estimated that ten graves were dug every one hundred miles to bury the dead. Most deaths occurred due to diseases caused by poor sanitation, such as cholera and typhoid fever. Another major cause of death for adults and children was falling off wagons and getting run over. Many pioneers purchased firearms for protection, the first weapons they had ever owned, and mishaps occurred, causing injury and death. Other deaths on the trail were due to drowning in rivers, suicide, weather, stampeding livestock, fellow migrant attacks, lightning and gunpowder explosions. Migrants became accustomed to death, suffering each loss together, quickly burying their dead and pressing on in hopes of a better life. There were some conflicts between Natives and migrants along the trail, but they were relatively rare. It is estimated that between 1840 and 1860, Natives killed 362 migrants and migrants killed 426 Natives. As might be expected based on the suffering and deaths along the Oregon Trail, ghost stories and reported sightings are plentiful.

Sylvester Park was donated to the city by Olympia cofounder Edmund Sylvester in 1850. Sheep grazed at the park in the early years. Sylvester was from Maine and wanted the park to look like an old-fashioned New England town square (I'm originally from New England, and it does). The park, like the rest of the Oregon Trail, is said to be haunted, with full-body apparitions in old-fashioned clothing seen moving about. Another reason the park may be haunted is that during the Puget Sound War of 1855–56, Olympia residents fled to the park for protection from impending (they believed) attack by the

Natives. There were forts and blockhouses at the park (in which Native Chief Leschi was imprisoned, prior to his hanging in 1858), and the U.S. military handed out weapons and ammunition to locals. Interestingly, no attack came, and there were no deaths reported in the park due to it being part of the Oregon Trail or to the Puget Sound War. However, as I've explained in previous books, hauntings and other supernatural phenomena are reported at locations that suffered trauma (if not deaths). The first example I've cited is Fort Stevens (built in 1863) in Warrenton, Oregon, which in 1942 became the only contiguous U.S. military base attacked since the War of 1812 by a foreign power (a Japanese submarine lobbed missiles into the base). No one was killed; however, those present described the scene as a "madhouse," and ghosts in Civil War and World War II clothing have been reported there ever since. The second example is Starvation Pass in the Columbia River Gorge. There, in 1885, a train trying to make its way to Portland, Oregon, was blocked by snow from a recent storm. Riders had to burn their wooden seats for warmth, and some had to walk through the snow to complete their journey (a traumatic event, to be sure). Again, no one died, but the gorge's reported paranormal climate is said to be tied, in part, to traumatic events like this.

The Avanti High School of Olympia (first known as the Old Washington School) opened in 1924. Since the late 1950s, people have reported a haunting by a worker's spirit—it is said he was painting a railing near a fourth-floor window when he slipped and fell to his death. Witnesses have described how his ghost shuts windows and doors and has made people who visit the fourth floor uncomfortable. Creeped-out students report hearing, after school hours, sounds echoing down hallways, disembodied footsteps and voices and catching a glimpse of movement in the corner of their eye at the far ends of hallways. A fun haunted house is held at the school each year.

The historic and Gothic Bigelow House mansion and museum was built during the 1850s and is the oldest house in Olympia. Employees closing for the evening have reported seeing the apparition of a distinguished gentleman scrutinizing the displays who vanishes when approached. They believe it is the ghost of Daniel Bigelow, the pioneer lawyer and politician who contributed to the creation of the pre-statehood Washington Territory in 1854, died in 1905 at the age of eighty-one and once lived in the mansion. He was the last surviving member of the first Washington Territorial Legislature.

The Brotherhood Lounge was built in 1890 and lies beneath an old union hall (Olympia in the late nineteenth century was home to loggers, longshoremen, railroad workers and other union members), with a sign outside that reads "Labor Temple" (which is why it is called the Brotherhood).

Daniel T. Bigelow house in Olympia, Washington, 1933. *Courtesy of Library of Congress, Historic American Buildings Survey.*

Its nickname is Broho. The once-ornate façade was heavily damaged in a 1949 earthquake. The lounge is decorated with photographs of President John F. Kennedy and actor Bruce Lee, as well as a reproduction of grunge rocker Kurt Cobain's guitars (Cobain once lived in Olympia). The lounge is rumored to be the home of a friendly spirit, with whom staff have communicated. One employee reported seeing shadows of people on the wall late at night, although there was no one else present. Another employee closing the lounge late at night heard her name repeatedly whispered in her ear, even though no one was there.

Olympia's Capitol House Apartments on Sherman Street served as St. Peter's Hospital from the late 1880s to 1923; it was later expanded and renamed the Sherman Street Hospital (it existed until the 1960s). The building is said to be home to many ghosts. One longtime apartment resident described seeing an elderly lady casually rocking back and forth in a rocking chair in the lobby. As she approached the chair, a friend came out the door and called her name. The resident said she looked at her friend, then quickly looked back at the rocking chair, but both the rocking chair and elderly lady were inexplicably gone. She later explained that as the building had previously served as a hospital and many people no doubt died there, she was sure she had seen a ghost. Another apartment resident commented, "It's an old hospital; people died here all the time. I'm sure it's haunted. I've seen a ghost."

The Capitol Theater, built in 1924, served early on as an Odd Fellows Lodge (the Independent Order of Odd Fellows is a charitable fraternal organization). Later, it was a movie palace and vaudeville hall, playing host to various shows and programs. A 1937 fire caused extensive damage to the interior, much of which was replaced. There's a story about a murder taking place in the theater in the 1930s or '40s. Stories of multiple ghosts resulted in the ghost-hunting organization Paranormal Investigations of Historic America (PIHA) setting up its equipment and investigating the theater in 2010 (you can watch the investigation on YouTube). PIHA later certified the theater as "haunted." It found ghostly orbs, disembodied voices and electronic impulses, making use of electronic voice phenomena (EVP) and electromagnetic field (EMF) devices. The group found spirits in the theater's green room, dressing room and mezzanine. Probably the best-known ghost at the theater is the spirit of an elderly movie lover who is said to have died in the theater, sitting in an upper back balcony seat. He is said to disappear or dissipate when approached.

At the Georgia Pacific manufacturing building in Olympia, built in 1952, people have reported seeing the ghost of an elderly man walking in the offices above the production floor, sometimes walking through walls. Employees have reported shadow figures moving about in the facility after closing. Further, a blob-shaped entity was observed floating up to the ceiling. Lastly, an employee reported a disembodied voice answering them when they were talking to themselves in the customer service area.

The 1908 governor's mansion is the oldest building on the twelve-acre Washington Capitol campus. The mansion was originally designed as a temporary structure. Earthquakes in 1949 and 2001 caused damage to the building. In 1997, Governor Gary Locke and his family were forced to relocate temporarily to a nearby private residence (and to undergo rabies vaccinations) after an infestation of bats in the governor's mansion. But the bats were not the only creepy things reported in the building. The paranormal phenomena reported in the governor's mansion includes the apparition of a small boy wearing a blue sailor suit and riding an antique tricycle and the sound of a bouncing ball in hallways. In the 1960s, a tour group reportedly saw the child on his tricycle and even waved at him. Later, the group heard the bouncing ball. When members of the group asked about the child, their guide initially refused to answer and only later confessed that the mansion was haunted by the spirits of *two* little boys. The apparition of the boy with the tricycle seems to have disappeared after the extensive remodeling of the governor's mansion in the 1970s, but the sound of the bouncing ball reportedly persists. Witnesses report seeing the boy's ghost out of the corner of their eye, often in the bedroom or the lobby. He has also been reported riding past the fences on the capitol campus and haunting the man-made Capitol Lake and other parts of the campus. All six of the governors who resided in the mansion from 1909 to World War II had children (a total of twenty-one), although some of those children may have already grown to adulthood by the time their father became governor. It does not appear that any young children died while living in the governor's mansion during this time. It is therefore not clear who the ghost may have been in life.

The J.A. Denn Powder Company was in Olympia in 1934 (in what is now the Hawk's Prairie area of nearby Lacey). On June 27, 1934, the dynamite factory suffered an explosion that was heard and felt some twenty miles to the north in Tacoma. Eleven people died, ten male employees and a nearby female resident named Hazel Epley (who was reportedly thrown one hundred feet into the air). The Travel Channel program *Dead Files* (season 8, episode 7) tells the story of Hazel Epley's poltergeist haunting the area, harming the living (hitting and scratching some residents and contributing to the suicide of a young man). In addition to Hazel, other confused ghosts have been reported, milling about as if they don't know what happened.

Olympia's Old State Capitol Building was built in 1892 as the Thurston County Courthouse and served as the state's first capitol from 1905 to 1928. It continues to serve as the headquarters of the Washington Office of Superintendent of Public Instruction. Its nickname was the Castle, as it was reminiscent of such a building. The four-story, nineteen-room building was designed in the Georgian style with white pillars and a redbrick exterior trimmed with marble and sandstone. The building's large, 150-foot-tall central clock tower with illuminated clocks on each of its eight sides (residents said they could see it from a far distance) was destroyed by fire in 1928. The original turrets were toppled in the 1949 earthquake, with ten of twelve towers as well as the rotunda and house chamber damaged beyond repair. The renovated building that remains, still impressive, is known as one of the most haunted historic buildings in town. It is said that the Olympia Police are frequently summoned to the building at night, with security systems indicating an intruder—yet none is ever found. Two Olympia police officers experienced haunted entities, one reportedly getting the "willies" there at night. The other officer is said to have commented, "Ask any of the night staff [about the hauntings]; they'll tell you." A participant in one of my tours who had worked in the building agreed it (especially the basement) is "creepy."

The Spar Café was built in 1935 and is said to look just like it did when it opened. It is owned by McMenamin's, which is known in some circles as the haunted hotel and restaurant chain. It owns forty-six businesses in Oregon and ten in Washington, including two that frequently make "most haunted" lists: the White Eagle Saloon in Portland, Oregon, and the Edgefield in Troutdale, Oregon. Employees and visitors report "being watched" by unseen, nonhuman entities, being touched by someone or something that is not physically present and seeing items move on their own. Under the Spar is a tunnel rumored to have been used during Prohibition (when from 1920 to 1933, under the Eighteenth Amendment to the Constitution, the manufacture, sale and transportation of alcohol was prohibited in the United States) to transport alcohol to the Old State Capitol Building. One employee told me the basement, where the tunnel is located, is "creepy," and if the building is haunted, "that's where the ghosts are." There is also an artesian well in the basement.

Like the Capitol Theater, the State Theater, built in 1949, is said to be haunted. The building was previously the site of the fifth Thurston County courthouse and jail, where prisoners were kept awaiting trial. As with many old theaters, there is a ghost lamp on stage (some say to protect the living from injury, others say to scare away ghosts). Employees and visitors have reported strange movements even when no one else is present; strange, disembodied noises; and cold spots. Some believe theaters like the State and the Capitol are haunted, as they are locations where high energy and emotions were expressed and great success was achieved and because of their cavernous ambiance. (Having participated in community theater in California, I can attest to the high energy and emotions expressed!) The building being a former jail no doubt contributed to the heightened energy and emotions experienced there and the ghostly entities that have been reported.

Some people believe Olympia's Forest Memorial Gardens Cemetery, founded in April 1857 (during the Victorian era), is the most haunted site in the city. In my book *Pacific Northwest Legends and Lore*, I discuss the Victorians' strange death-related practices (e.g., carrying the dead body out of the home feetfirst so it couldn't beckon the living to follow it). Full-body apparitions milling about the tombstones, disembodied footsteps and voices, cold spots and temperature changes have all been detected at the cemetery. Many of Olympia's pioneer families are buried there, and it was the city's potter's field, where the unknown and unclaimed bodies of the destitute, immigrants and others were buried. Cemeteries—along with prisons, military bases, battlefields, some hotels and other places—are hotbeds of reported ghostly activity.

USS *Olympia*, 1895. *Courtesy of Library of Congress, Detroit Publishing Co.*

About three thousand miles east of Olympia, in Philadelphia, Pennsylvania, is docked the city's namesake ship, the USS *Olympia*. The ship was commissioned in 1885 and is the United States' oldest preserved steel warship, the last one from the Spanish-American War (1898). It served as Commodore George Dewey's flagship, and it was onboard that Dewey uttered the famous phrase "You may fire when ready, Gridley" during the crucial Battle of Manila (Philippines) Bay. Charles Vernon Gridley was the captain of the USS *Olympia*, and Dewey was instructing him to fire on the Spanish fleet. The ship, in service until 1922, saw action in World War I while protecting merchant ships from German U-boats. The USS *Olympia* is said to be one of the United States' most haunted ships; nineteen men died onboard over the years. Ghost tours are conducted on the ship, and visitors report an apparition in the engine room that grabs people. They also report phantom faces in mirrors, faceless ghosts roaming the halls and disembodied voices. The most famous ghost is that of Gunner Johnson, who was killed in a training accident.

Based on its many hauntings, Olympia may be not just the capital of Washington but also the capital of haunts.

CHAPTER 6

COMMUNITIES NEAR OLYMPIA

In southernmost Washington, close to Olympia and Puget Sound, are many small, rural, bucolic towns with haunted histories of their own. Many of these towns sponsor haunted houses and other Halloween events celebrating their ghostly history. I've visited many of them, and they truly hold their own in the scary story department. I describe some of these locations in this chapter.

The ghost town of Bordeaux sits fifteen minutes south of Olympia, set among the spooky and mysterious Mima Mounds (small, irregularly spaced hills—described by some as "soil pimples" because they are piles of silt, sand and pebbles—found throughout the southern Puget Sound whose origins are unknown). The town was built in the early 1900s and served as a busy lumber town for decades. By 1941, Bordeaux had a school, a post office, a lumber mill and a railroad leading to and from the surrounding forests. The lumber industry eventually took a downward turn, the mill closed and the townspeople moved on. All that remains of the town are several brick, wood and concrete structures. People who explore the abandoned area describe full-body apparitions of timber workers walking between their old workstations and what was the bank vault in search of their wages.

The small town of Bucoda, population 562, lies twenty miles south of Olympia. Its original name was Seatco, a Native American word meaning "evil spirit" or "devil." In October each year, the small town embraces its haunted history and becomes "Boo-coda," a destination for Halloween lovers. Bucoda holds casket races, hearse processions, a zombie 5K race,

Statue of Meriwether
Lewis. *By Photoman
via Pixabay.*

jack-o'-lantern carving contests, "Thriller" dance lessons (based on Michael
Jackson's hit song and video), pumpkin pancake–eating events and a haunted
house. However, Bucoda's history may be scarier than the modern-day
Halloween events it holds. A resident once reported seeing a transparent figure
wearing striped prisoner's clothing; the town was the site of Washington's
first territorial prison, reported to be a brutal facility, from 1874 to 1888. In
fact, the facility's nickname was Hell on Earth. Also, in 2009, the story goes
that Bucoda contracted a painter to work on the haunted house—which is
run inside an old gym, originally built in the 1930s, that is said to be the site
of three deaths. Late one night, the artist was painting the image of a little
girl on the wall. Suddenly, he heard giggling. He got up and looked around,
but nobody was there. He thought he must have misheard, so he got back to
work and tried to think of something else. Just as his heart rate had begun
to settle, right behind him, he heard a voice whisper: "*Boo.*" Again, the
disembodied sound led him to search the area—but he was alone. He later
told town officials that he would never work alone in that building again.
Locals view the spirit as energetic but harmless. In April 2011, paranormal
investigators investigated the Bucoda Gym and found ghostly orbs.

In Centralia, twenty-two miles south of Olympia, the historic Olympic
Club Hotel and saloon, built in 1908, is said to have been the scene of
several murders. Employees have reported seeing ghostly orbs, shadows of
people who aren't there and mist or ectoplasm throughout the hotel and
hearing disembodied voices, footsteps and the sounds of other movements
emanating from vacant rooms.

In between Olympia and Tacoma to the north lies the sprawling military
Joint Base Lewis-McChord (JBLM)—named in part for American explorer

Meriwether Lewis—created when the U.S. Army's Fort Lewis and the U.S. Air Force's McChord base merged in 2010. It is a training and mobilization center and the only army power projection base (with pre-positioned military units and weapons strategically placed for use elsewhere) within the continental United States west of the Rocky Mountains. The base is descended from earlier bases dating to the mid-nineteenth century used to quell hostilities between Natives and settlers traveling the Oregon Trail. The base is said to be home to not only airmen and soldiers but also to several spirits. Some have reported hearing the cries of Natives who were forced to leave their land. Others have reported hearing disembodied chanting and singing at odd hours of the night. Others still report the sounds of unseen marching soldiers. One story has it that in 1927, during the filming of the World War I–based silent movie *The Patent Leather Kid*, a movie worker was murdered on the second floor of what is now the military museum and was formerly the historic Red Shield Inn. After that, a cowboy's sad or angry spirit was frequently seen in the area, accompanied by disembodied sounds, crying, cold spots and alarms going off for no apparent reason. It is said that building management summoned three priests to the building to perform an exorcism, during which, the priests said, a man's apparition appeared before them, claiming he was distraught because he had caused his own death. The priests gave him forgiveness and permission to leave, and the cowboy's ghost faded away.

McNeil Island (nicknamed the Alcatraz of the Pacific Northwest after the infamous island prison in the San Francisco Bay) is an island west of Steilacoom, in between Olympia and Tacoma. For much of its history, it served as a fishing location for Coastal Salish Natives. In 1841, it was named for the captain of the Hudson Bay Company's steamers *Beaver*, *Llama* and *Una*, William Henry McNeill. From 1875 to 1976, McNeil Island served as a federal penitentiary. By 1947, its population was 320 inmates. Well-known inmates included, from 1909 to 1912, Robert "Birdman of Alcatraz" Stroud, for manslaughter, and from 1961 to 1966, future mass murderer (to take place in 1971 in California) Charles Manson for forgery. From 1981 to 2011, the island served as a state correctional facility. It now serves as a state special commitment center, confining over one hundred dangerous sexual predators. A social worker who worked with prisoners at the facility took one of my history and haunted nautical tours and described the island and the buildings on it as "spooky" and haunted. Many prisons are said to be haunted, presumably based on the misery and anger taking place there, by lingering spirits, ghostly footsteps, disembodied voices and noises, screams and eerie music. Interestingly, Charles Manson's bone fragments, the hospital gown he was wearing when he died and his coroner's toe tag are maintained at the Travel Channel's *Ghost Adventures* host Zak Bagans's Haunted Museum in Las Vegas. Creepy!

Twenty miles northeast of Olympia lies the town of Steilacoom. It was one of the earliest non-Native settlements in what would become Washington State and the first town to incorporate in 1854. It served as a hub of social and economic activity until the 1870s, when the railroad passed it by. The Captain Edwin R. Rogers mansion was built in Steilacoom in 1891 by Rogers, a wealthy sea merchant, for himself; his wife, Catherine; and their large family. Unfortunately, Rogers lost most of his fortune in the 1893 recession and was only able to live in the mansion for two years. In 1920, the mansion became the Waverly Hotel. In subsequent years, it served as a museum, then as the E.R. Rogers Restaurant. In 2006, the mansion was beautifully restored and now serves as home to law firms. Allegedly, the mansion is haunted by several spirits. Chief Leschi was hanged in 1858 on a gallows near the property, and his spirit has been seen standing and looking out at Puget Sound. Sometime during the Waverly Hotel years, a male guest is said to have been mugged and killed, and his ghost has reportedly been seen looking out at the sound. Another male spirit is thought to be that of E.R. Rogers himself, still attached to the mansion he built but lived in only briefly. There is also a female spirit thought to be that of Hattie Bair, the wife of Warren L. Bair, who owned Bair Drug and Hardware (his ghost is said to be attached to that building). She has been seen wearing a white dress and floating near the ceiling of the restaurant's lavish second-floor bar. Employees and guests have reported hearing her footsteps and seeing a pair of disembodied women's legs in stockings. Mirrors and windows have reflected parts of an elegantly dressed woman wearing an old-fashioned dress and hairstyle. The apparition of a man who died in a fight on the mansion grounds has allegedly been seen ascending an invisible staircase. There have been unexplained electrical surges in the mansion, and unseen feet have left imprints in the carpet. Lights and the security system have come on by themselves, and candles and glasses have been thrown off tables by unseen hands. Also in Steilacoom, the Bair Drug and Hardware Store Museum, a historic pharmacy, general store, museum and bistro, dates to 1908. Staff and diners say the ghost of former owner W.L. Bair haunts it, shattering glasses, rearranging cutlery and playing with electrical appliances.

Although small, these towns near Olympia have big ghost stories to tell.

CHAPTER 7

TACOMA

Tacoma (2021 population 219,205) is the county seat of Pierce County (2021 population 925,708). A port city, it is located along Puget Sound thirty-four miles southwest of Seattle, thirty-one miles northeast of Olympia and fifty-eight miles northwest of Mount Rainier National Park. Tacoma is the second-largest city (by population) in the Puget Sound region, the third largest in the state and a center of business activity. Its nicknames include Grit City and the Pretty Gritty City (I work with Pretty Gritty Tours of Tacoma leading tours of nearby Olympia) due to its lovely waterfront location and blue-collar, hardscrabble roots. It is an evolving cultural and technological center and is known for its world-famous glass art (including the Museum of Glass).

The Puyallup Native people lived in settlements on the delta for centuries. The first non-Native resident, Swedish settler Nicholas De Lin, arrived in 1852, and he later built the region's first sawmill. The city grew and was named Tacoma City, derived from the Native name for a nearby mountain. Tacoma was incorporated in 1875, following its 1873 selection as the westernmost termination point of the Northern Pacific Railroad, and its population grew from just over one thousand in 1880 to over thirty-six thousand in 1890. Based on the railroad's presence, the city's motto became "when rail meets sail" and its nickname the "City of Destiny." Tacoma's neighboring deep-water harbor, Commencement Bay, influenced the railroad's decision to build tracks to the city. British author Rudyard

Bird's-eye view of Tacoma and Mount Rainier, Washington Territory, 1878. *Courtesy of Library of Congress, E.S. Glover and A.L. Bancroft & Company.*

Kipling (of *Jungle Book* fame) visited Tacoma in 1889 and described it as the "boomiest" of cities, meaning it was developing rapidly. In 1940, the city gained notoriety due to the collapse of the Tacoma Narrows Bridge, otherwise known as Galloping Gertie, due to the bridge's wild movements in high wind, which also caused it to collapse.

From the 1880s to the 1920s in the Puget Sound region, two million people a year traveled aboard wooden steamboats called the Mosquito Fleet. The boats stopped at virtually every waterfront dock and were often jerry-rigged and occasionally less than seaworthy. Before depth sonar and GPS (global positioning systems), collisions and other accidents were not uncommon. Sudden, unexpected deaths and destruction caused by shipwrecks are connected to reported local paranormal and supernatural events. There were seventy-three shipwrecks in Puget Sound; I describe several in the following pages.

The worst shipwreck on Puget Sound involved the *Dix*, a 102-foot, 130-ton vessel that wrecked on November 18, 1906. That day, the ship steamed from the Seattle dock to Bainbridge Island with seventy-seven onboard. The *Dix* was piloted by a confused and unlicensed ship's first officer by the name of Charles Dennison. Captain Percy Lermond was collecting fares (a task many ship captains did). There was no lookout watching for obstacles, and two miles west of Alki, the first officer steered the Mosquito Fleet steamer into the much larger four-masted steam schooner *Jeanie* (186 feet long, 1,000 tons). The *Dix* rolled like a log, split in two and sank within five minutes, killing forty-five of the seventy-seven onboard. It was a starry night, and the *Dix*'s speed was slow, but the ship was top-heavy. The wreck remains six hundred feet underwater in Puget Sound; victims' bodies were never recovered, nor were pieces of the vessel. This was Puget Sound's worst maritime disaster and Washington's second-worst transportation disaster, behind the 1910 Wellington train wreck at Stevens Pass that killed ninety-six passengers. The *Dix*'s captain survived, and his license was revoked—later to be reinstated but only to captain cargo ships.

In my upcoming book *Pacific Northwest Legends and Lore*, I write about the curses related to Tacoma's largest shipwreck—the *Andelana*, a 304-foot, four-masted British barque or large sailing ship. It docked in Tacoma, Washington's Commencement Bay on January 13, 1899. I describe the ghost stories related to the wreck here.

The *Andelana*'s crew thought the ship, with its unusually tall masts, was unstable on the water, and for this reason, they wanted off the ship. Nine crew members did successfully get off the ship in Tacoma, but the captain wouldn't allow the remaining seventeen to leave. Furthermore, the captain had a photo taken of the remaining crew members with their dogs to intimidate them (as if to say, "I know who you are—don't you dare leave"). Twenty-four hours later, all seventeen were dead, having been trapped in their sleeping quarters when the ship sank. The *Andelana* was top-heavy, with no ballast in its hold to stabilize the ship as it awaited a shipment of wheat bound for Europe. A freak storm raced across Commencement Bay, with forty-mile-per-hour gusts, and capsized the ship in two hundred feet of water. A diver attempted to reach the *Andelana* in 1935, but the leather seal attaching his suit to oxygen ruptured, causing him to be crushed to death (the eighteenth human death related to this disaster). The *Andelana* has never been raised.

Several ghostly occurrences related to the sinking of the *Andelana* have been reported. A note in a bottle purportedly written by one of the *Andelana*'s seventeen doomed sailors and dated two days *after* the sinking washed up decades later on a beach in Mexico. Research into messages in bottles shows they are often sent as distress messages. Furthermore, the chances of finding a message in a bottle are roughly equivalent to those of winning the lottery. Was this a note from the dead appealing for help, a misdated message or something else altogether?

In another ghostly occurrence related to the *Andelana*, visitors to the Port of Tacoma (the city's working waterfront) and Tacoma's Commencement

Tacoma, Washington Harbor, 1908. *Courtesy of Library of Congress, U.S. Geog. File.*

Bay claim to have repeatedly seen a ghostly rowboat disappear into the water and swimmers suddenly vanish into the fog at about the same location where the *Andelana* sank. Disembodied voices and cries for help have also been reported at that location. Finally, ghost ships (ships controlled by the undead who died in an accident or wreck or suffered a sudden and unexpected end) have been reported in the waters of Puget Sound, of which Commencement Bay is a part. One of those ghost ships is thought to be the doomed *Andelana*. It appears the spirits of the drowned sailors and those who perished trying to reach the wreck are not resting peacefully!

The next year, in 1900, another disaster struck Tacoma when the United States' worst streetcar crash took place on July 4. Tacoma Railway & Power Company's streetcar no. 55 malfunctioned, and riders awaited the next vehicle. At eight o'clock in the morning, streetcar no. 116 pulled away from the stop in South Tacoma heading downtown. The Independence Day parade was expected to attract over 50,000 people. The streetcar was designed to hold 55 passengers, but about 150 people (some standing on the running boards, others hanging from the railings) crowded onboard. The passengers weighed in at roughly fourteen thousand pounds, or seven tons. Conditions were wet as the streetcar descended the Delin Street hill toward a sharp curve. Motorman F.L. Boehm (on the job less than a month) tried putting the electric engine in reverse but could not slow the overloaded vehicle. This was the fastest many of the passengers had ever gone (at a time before most had ridden in cars), as the streetcar was traveling at fifty miles per hour instead of its usual ten. Passengers began to jump off, but many could not, as they were wedged into the vehicle. The tracks curved onto a trestle at C Street (now Commerce Street), near the intersection of South Twenty-Sixth and C Streets, and the vehicle left the tracks, jumped a guardrail intended as a safety feature and plunged over one hundred feet into Gallagher's Gulch (now South Tacoma Way). The streetcar's ruptured steel and spraying glass caused catastrophic damage to riders. It landed upside down at the bottom of the ravine, with the bodies of the dead either catapulted yards away or still stuck in the wreckage. Police officers preparing for duty during the Independence Day parade, residents and those nearby heard the horrific crashing noise and attempted to provide aid to the victims. They described the scene as horrific, with 44 dead and over 70 seriously

Streetcar, 1900. *Courtesy of Library of Congress.*

injured. The following investigation and jury trial found the motorman responsible for allowing the streetcar to reach excessive speeds. They further found the company criminally negligent for assigning motorman Boehm an unfamiliar route and for improper maintenance of its cars and rails and the unsafe grade. Boehm testified that he might have been able to safely negotiate the curve if the streetcar hadn't been overloaded. The company stopped using the trestle shortly thereafter, and it was torn down in 1910. By 1938, streetcars had been replaced by buses and other means of transportation. Disaster sites such as this are often reported to be haunted by those who experienced such a sudden and horrible end. One can sense, when visiting this site, the spirits of those who lost their lives in the United States' worst streetcar disaster, on their way to what should have been a happy event.

The Pantages Theater is the centerpiece of Tacoma's historic Theater District. The theater was constructed in 1918 and since that time has been reported to have regular ghostly visitors. Alexander Pantages built the theater; he was an early movie producer and theater entrepreneur. His mistress, the beautiful and wealthy Kate Klondike, paid for the Pantages, investing all her money in an effort to demonstrate her love for Alexander. Nonetheless, Alexander left Kate for another woman, leaving her emotionally devastated and destitute until her death. Alexander's and Kate's spirits are believed to haunt the theater to this day, visiting different parts of the building. While Kate's ghost seems to haunt only the Tacoma Pantages, Alexander's spirit is thought to visit both Tacoma's Pantages and his other prized Pantages properties in Hollywood, California. In addition, there are other apparitions said to haunt the Tacoma Pantages. Visitors and employees report seeing a ghostly female in the balcony. This spirit is said to dress in elegant Vaudeville-era clothing, sing ballads in Italian and make eye contact with the living before dissipating. Theatergoers arriving late for a show have described being escorted by a blurry figure in an usher's uniform who walks them—with his cold, lifeless hand on their shoulder—to their seat. He has also been known, when guests reach their assigned row, to stop them "dead in their tracks."

Point Defiance Park lies six miles from Tacoma and is home to over ten miles of trails, a zoo and an aquarium and the historic fort. Five Mile Drive, in the park, is said to be home to the ghost of Jennifer Marie Bastian, a twelve-year-old girl who disappeared in August 1986 while riding her bike at the park. Her body was discovered later by joggers just off Five Mile Drive, but the killer was never identified or caught. Several people have said they've seen a girl riding her bike alone on the darker, quieter stretches of the road

Point Defiance Park, Tacoma, Washington, 1906. *Courtesy of Library of Congress.*

and trail who vanishes when they get close to her. It is said Jennifer's bike can be heard on Five Mile Drive in the dead of night. One witness reported seeing the girl's eerily smiling ghost—but she had no eyes. Another spirit roaming the park is said to be that of a man who may have committed suicide after his wife drowned in the lake. The pagoda seems to be a hot spot for spectral and paranormal activity: people have reported seeing shadows, hearing disembodied footsteps and sighing and feeling inexplicable cold drafts. The reported spirits are most prevalent in the early morning hours and on cloudy, misty days late in the day. I've visited the park and, as I often do, watched for anything out of the ordinary and possibly supernatural.

People walking around the mouth of the Puyallup River in Tacoma report seeing the spirit of a homeless man in torn clothes with a deep scowl on his face. He acknowledges passersby, then disappears. In the late 1920s and 1930s, during the Great Depression, this area on the tideflats was the site of a large homeless encampment. Such encampments were termed shantytowns and Hoovervilles, for former President Herbert Hoover, due to his perceived inability to provide economic relief. Tacoma city officials struggled to control the area's rising indigent population, burning down more than fifty of their shacks in 1942 to chase them out. Many of these people rebuilt their shacks and lived in that section of town for another ten years. The final resident took his own life during an altercation with the police, who had been sent to remove him. It is thought the apparition is that of the homeless man who committed suicide and is forever haunting his old home.

Stadium High School is known for being featured in the 1990s movie *10 Things I Hate About You*. However, its reportedly supernatural connection may be of greatest appeal to those interested in the paranormal. The school was originally built in the late 1800s but not as a school; rather, it was to be the Pacific Northwest's and Tacoma's grandest and most ornate hotel. The timing was not good; just as the building was completed, the financial Panic of 1893 struck, forcing a stop to construction. The huge building was used as a warehouse for lumber for several years. In 1896, a fire gutted the structure. Following repairs, the building was nicknamed Brown's Castle. It sat on a hill overlooking Tacoma's Commencement Bay and the ravine beneath it, which townsfolk referred to as Old Woman's Gulch because of the shacks on Puget Sound's shore that served as homes for widows of sailors who would never come home from the sea. As the story goes, the widows remained in the shacks, living out the rest of their lives, watching and hoping for their men to return—but sometimes jumping to their death. In present times, faculty and students have reported a woman in black looking out over Old Woman's Gulch. The woman's ghost is seen for only a few seconds before leaping off the cliff and disappearing.

Tacoma's vacant Old City Hall, built in 1893, which served as the city's government headquarters for fifty years, is reported to be one of the most haunted sites in Washington. The building has been largely vacant since the 1950s and is said to be home to a trickster ghost named Gus who moves elevators between floors, turns lights on and off, sets off fire and intruder alarms, locks and unlocks doors and throws objects. On investigating these incidents, police find no evidence of a human intruder. At a restaurant that was temporarily operating on the building's first floor, frequented by lawyers and politicians, Gus was reportedly seen knocking bottles of alcohol off the shelves, only to then line them up on the counter in front of the startled onlookers. He was seen breaking dishes and glasses and rattling silverware. It's thought that Gus may be the ghost of an inmate who, along with other criminals, was housed in the building's jail at the beginning of the twentieth century. It's also common for the Old City Hall's clock tower bell to ring late at night or early in the morning, even though the building is empty. Security guards have reported seeing floating shadowy apparitions on various floors of the building and outside the old council chambers, and the sound of someone coughing can be heard when there is no one around.

Downtown Tacoma is home to one of the strangest and most awe-inspiring spirits in the area (and I find this story fascinating). Down the hill from the Pantages Theater once stood the Tacoma Hotel. The hotel was built in 1884 (and burned down in 1935) to serve Tacoma's best-known and richest visitors. President Theodore Roosevelt, baseball player Babe Ruth and author Mark Twain were some of the hotel's best-known guests, but the Tacoma Hotel was also home to another unique guest (or, some may say, staff member), Jack, an eight-hundred-pound brown bear who was the hotel's pet. Jack's mother was killed by hunters, who took Jack home and raised him as a pet. The hotel had a Bear Garden where Jack was kept. His handlers gave him a bath every morning in the French hogshead (shaped like a hog's snout) bathtub, then served him a cocktail along with his breakfast. Jack casually stood on his back legs leaning against the wall while he was served a Manhattan, or he would sit at the bar, just like any other guest, and drink a beer. After a while, Jack would walk through the hotel to the billiards room as guests watched in amazement. Jack was always relaxed, friendly and unbothered by the drunken guests who would poke at the gentle creature. But occasionally, Jack would escape his collar and enclosure at night and take a stroll through the streets of Tacoma—a frightening thought! One night, in the 1880s, on one of Jack's strolls down Pacific Avenue, a rookie policeman (who didn't know Jack's story) mistook him for dangerous and shot him twice in the side. Jack later died from his wounds, and the hotel's staff and patrons carried his body back to the Tacoma Hotel. Jack's stuffed remains were kept outside the hotel's dining room for years, where he greeted visitors. Later, his body was given to the Washington State History Museum. Finally, in 1958, Jack's remains were given away, and their current whereabouts are unknown. Some people in Tacoma have reported seeing Jack's spirit wandering through downtown in the late hours of the night or early hours of the morning before dissipating into the darkness. Witnesses are left stunned by what they've seen.

At the University of Puget Sound, Schiff Hall in particular, there are paranormal stories centered on Ted Bundy, a serial killer (someone who murders individuals at different times, as opposed to a mass murderer, who typically kills multiple people at the same time) who may have possibly lived there (while attending school); other stories say he lived at home. Bundy graduated from Tacoma's Woodrow Wilson High School before enrolling in the university. He transferred to the University of Washington in Seattle and later attended the University of Puget Sound's law school for one year. Soon after, Bundy, oddly (given his murderous activities) was employed as the assistant director of the Seattle Crime Prevention Advisory Commission (the proverbial fox in the henhouse). It was around that time that women started disappearing in the Pacific Northwest. According to one story, the apparition of an eight-year-old girl, Ann Marie Burr, who in 1961 disappeared from her bedroom a few blocks away, haunts Schiff Hall. All that was found at her house was a man's shoe print on the porch. The story goes that Bundy murdered Ann Marie and dumped her body into Schiff Hall's foundation as it was being built. Students report that the spirit lingers around dark corners; they have heard shuffling feet and seen a trail of wet slipper marks on the floor that suddenly ends. In 1989, Bundy was executed after confessing to thirty-six gruesome murders (we may never know the exact number of people he killed; it may have been much higher), but he always denied being involved in Ann Marie's death. Other stories involve bodies hidden in the walls of the dorm, in abandoned elevator shafts, deep under the basement and under dorm rooms. There are stories of wailing or crying coming from empty rooms. Some people say there are weird symbols or markings on the back of the sign welcoming drivers as they drive onto the university grounds, suggesting a dark and indecipherable warning. Making the story even creepier is that Bundy said an "entity" would "come over him" when he committed his crimes. Bundy may also have lived in Olympia, and his ghost may still be present. If Bundy did live in Olympia, it may have been at the Cooper's Glen apartments (now called Evergreen Garden). A comment on the website ApartmentRatings reads: "[Ted Bundy's] ghost haunts" Evergreen Garden.

Tacoma surely is gritty, pretty and seemingly haunted.

CHAPTER 8

COMMUNITIES NEAR TACOMA

Tacoma is close to other smaller, rural, bucolic cities and towns in the mid-southern region of Washington, which have haunted histories of their own. I discuss some of them in this chapter.

Algona is a small city in King County with a population of 3,290 as of 2020. It was first settled by homesteaders in the 1870s and '80s and was incorporated years later, on August 22, 1955. The city lies some fifteen miles northeast of Tacoma, and the Old Hotel is the second-oldest building in town. Legend has it that a witch lived there, and she could not cast a shadow. Visitors to the Old Hotel today report sightings of her shadow (now apparently visible), black cats, disembodied voices and sounds, electrical disturbances and other anomalies occurring around the building.

Twenty-eight miles southeast of Tacoma is the Melmont Ghost Town, in Carbonado. There, the ruins of the former town lie in a foreboding manner alongside abandoned old cars. The town dates to the early twentieth century and was active in coal mining. The town had a train depot, saloon, butcher shop, hotel, store and Northern Pacific Railroad housing (self-segregated by nationality). By 1918, the railroad had switched from steam to diesel and electric power. Finally, in the 1920s, the town burned down. The remnants of the town are still visible, and one can imagine the townsfolk, miners and others going about their business there some one hundred years ago. The ghost town has been described as "spooky," and as in many ghost towns, some visitors have seen strange movements (when no one was else there) and heard disembodied voices

Ghost town. *By code83 via Pixabay.*

and other odd noises. I personally love visiting ghost towns and getting a sense of how people once lived and died there, whether they are virtually empty of life or touristy (like Virginia City, Nevada).

Graham is a rural area with grand views of nearby Mount Rainier. Its population was 32,658 in 2020, and it lies about twenty-three miles southeast of Tacoma. It is said a family was forced to move out of their home by an angry spirit. The ghost of an elderly woman lingers on the property where her husband died of a heart attack in 1994. A psychic told the family that the old woman doesn't realize she's dead. In a separate reported haunting in Graham, the ghost is said to be that of a young woman who was murdered while she was on a date. Legend has it she's exacting revenge by tormenting the man living in her former house.

In the early 1900s, in Olalla, twenty-five miles northwest of Tacoma, Dr. Linda Burfield and her husband, Sam Hazzard, ran Starvation Heights Sanitarium. They believed fasting was therapeutic and treated illnesses with extreme starvation. More than forty patients died because of this ineffective and dangerous treatment, including withholding food. Linda was also convicted of forging patients' wills and stealing their valuables. All that remains of the sanitarium is the building's foundation, as well as the incinerator where the dead were cremated. Ghosts of patients are said to haunt the grounds, including young boys Jeff and Kyle. Starvation Heights, as it's called, has been discussed on season 4 of the Travel Channel's *Ghost Hunters* and the Investigation Discovery Network's show *Deadly Women*. Dr. Hazzard maintained her positive public image as a strong female leader while dead patients' bodies were cremated in the sanitarium to cover up their mistreatment.

The sprawling and beautiful Gothic-Tudor style Thornewood Castle in Lakewood, ten miles southwest of Tacoma, was built in 1911 by Chester Thorne, a business magnate who was a founder of the Port of Tacoma. Thorne was one of the wealthiest men in Washington, also founding the National Bank of Tacoma and Mount Rainier Park. He was generous, donating money and supplies to people in need during the depression of 1893. Thornewood Castle—nicknamed "the house that love built"—was constructed over four years as a gift to Thorne's bride, Anna. Wanting the castle to be as authentic as possible, Thorne purchased a four-hundred-year-old English manor and had it painstakingly taken apart and shipped brick by brick to the United States onboard three ships sailing around Cape Horn. Thorne spared no expense in constructing the magnificent building, designed by famous architect Kirkland Cutter. At twenty thousand square feet, the castle now serves as an inn offering fifty-four rooms, including twenty-two bedrooms and bathrooms. It has a collection of rare hand-painted stained-glass artwork that is mounted in windows throughout the estate. The inn plays host to masquerade balls, Shakespearean plays and film screenings. There are also beautiful handcrafted fountains and gardens throughout the manor. The castle has been fully restored and is on the National Register of Historic Places.

Guests and employees have reported several ghosts at Thornewood Castle. One is said to be Chester Thorne himself, who turns lights in his former bedroom on the second floor on and off. He died in that bedroom from old age. Witnesses say Thorne's spirit walks through the front door of his room and past the bed, disappearing into his restroom. He has also been seen on the lawn and near the fountains, either riding his horse or standing in horseback-riding gear, holding a whip. Other witnesses report seeing the spirit of Thorne's wife, Anna, sitting in the window seat of her room on the second floor, looking longingly out at the garden. Anna's room, now the bridal suite, contains her former mirror, which has been said to sometimes hold her reflection looking at you from behind. Mysterious shadows of people who aren't there have been observed in the room, and the sounds of a grand piano have been heard. Employees and guests have reported seeing Chester and Anna standing with locked arms at the top of the staircase, dressed for an event, but they never move and vanish after a moment. Apparitions of two of the Thornes' three children have been reported: their eldest daughter sitting on the porch and their son standing on the lawn. One of the manor's former owners' grandchildren died (although some reports say it was the Thornes' son) by drowning in the 1970s, and his apparition has been seen standing by the lake. Guests report approaching the small child, only to find he has vanished. A ghostly cocktail party has been reported, with one hundred apparitions dancing, socializing and drinking. The castle's ghosts are described as mischievous, blowing out candles and unscrewing lightbulbs. Based on its reputedly haunted history, Thornewood Castle served as the filming location for the 2002 Stephen King television miniseries *Rose Red*, about a haunted mansion located in the Seattle area and built on top of a Native burial ground with a long history of supernatural events and unexplained tragedies.

Puyallup lies ten miles to the southeast of Tacoma and is the site of the Meeker Mansion, a seventeen-room Italianate Victorian mansion built in 1890 by pioneers Ezra Morgan and Eliza Jane Meeker. As a young man, Ezra traversed the Oregon Trail from Iowa to the Pacific Northwest by ox-drawn wagon. He grew hops for brewing beer and grew wealthy, becoming known as the Hop King of the World. Meeker served as the first mayor of Puyallup, from 1889 to 1891. Determined to remind the public of the importance of the Oregon Trail, from 1906 to 1908 and well into his seventies, Meeker retraced his journey. He met Presidents Theodore Roosevelt and Calvin Coolidge and other dignitaries. The house was later used as a hospital for a brief period. The Meeker Mansion is said to be haunted by the spirits of both Ezra and Eliza Meeker, who have been seen and heard sleeping in their old bedroom. Visitors who have spent the night say they heard Ezra's ghost snoring, while others say they saw him in the yard sawing logs. Both apparitions have been reported at social functions, only to vanish into thin air. People also claim to have smelled Eliza Meeker's ghostly perfume. The mansion has been restored and is operated by the Puyallup Historical Society.

These small towns, close to Tacoma, certainly pack a punch when it comes to ghost stories.

CHAPTER 9

SEATTLE

The Seattle area has been inhabited by Coastal Salish Natives, including the Duwamish, for at least four thousand years, living in some seventeen villages around Elliott Bay. In 1851, White settlers arrived and called the area New York but later changed it to Seattle in honor of Duwamish and Suquamish Native leader Chief Seattle (1786–1866), who had befriended and helped the settlers. Seattle—nicknamed the Emerald City—and the surrounding area are filled with greenery year-round. Seattle is Washington's (and the Pacific Northwest's) largest city, with a 2022 population of 749,256, and the northernmost major city in the United States. It is the United States' fifteenth-largest metropolitan area, with a population of over four million. It is sprawling (much more so than when I first visited it in the 1980s) and feels in many ways like other large cities like Los Angeles and Chicago in terms of its high population density. While beautiful, it, like many cities, has problems with homelessness, drugs and other modern challenges.

In the 1850s, Seattle produced lumber for San Francisco and towns in the Puget Sound area. In the 1870s, coal was discovered near Lake Washington, and the Northern Pacific Railway Company announced that it would build its westernmost point in Tacoma, forty miles south of Seattle. Mid-northern Washington (from Tacoma to Seattle) and the Puget Sound boomed, with logging, coal, fishing, trade and shipbuilding as the leading industries. Today, Seattle is headquarters for several leading companies, including Amazon, Costco, Microsoft and Starbucks.

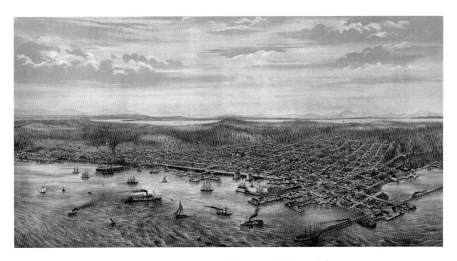

Bird's-eye view of Seattle, Washington, 1878. *Courtesy of Library of Congress.*

The Great Seattle Fire struck the city on June 6, 1889. The inferno started on Front Street and Madison Avenue, in the basement of Clairmont and Company's cabinet shop, when glue boiled over and ignited wood chips in a nearby carpentry shop. Fires in the Pacific Northwest (and elsewhere) were not uncommon in the late nineteenth century. Sidewalks and streets were made of wood (often planks on top of logs), as were most buildings; this was thought to be an improvement over earlier dirt paths and roads. Furthermore, fire departments weren't the professional organizations they are today and lacked adequate firefighting equipment. The fire caused millions of dollars in property damage and destroyed the entire twenty-five-block downtown area. Surprisingly, the fire itself claimed no human lives, although one million rats are thought to have died. However, the cleanup of the city after the fire led to the deaths of dozens of workers. It is those victims who are said to have left the biggest mark on the city they tried desperately to save. The ghosts of the dead workers are said to haunt the former business district (including Pioneer Square, described next), as evidenced by full-body apparitions, orbs, mist or ectoplasm, cold spots and temperature changes.

Below historic Pioneer Square, Seattle's original neighborhood, are tunnels that once comprised downtown Seattle. Downtown Seattle was built at sea level and was prone to flooding and sewage problems. Seattle's late-nineteenth-century sewage problems are fascinating on their own. Waste from outhouses (which were invented in fifteenth-century Europe) was washed into the streets by high tides, which caused unsanitary living

Pioneer Square, Seattle, Washington, 1915. *Courtesy of Library of Congress, August Cohn.*

conditions. Thomas Crapper (his real name—he was a British plumber and businessman) brought the "Crapper" or toilet to Seattle, impacting resident's everyday personal lives. As opposed to outhouses, the Crapper required a connection to the city's central sewage system, which Seattle lacked. In response, Seattle's first central sewage system was developed—an inadequate "pipe" made of elongated, connected box-shaped wood. Puget Sound's tide cycle and the flawed sewage drainage system caused great pressure, and the reversal of the wastewater shot up like a geyser, blowing users off the Crapper. There were many challenges in the development of Seattle's early wastewater system. The biggest problems related to the elevation of the city, the ebb and flow of the tides and the lack of city planning and adequate piping. These problems persisted until 1890, when the city burned down (in the great 1889 fire).

 As the city was rebuilt, the street level was raised two stories, creating a labyrinth of underground storefronts and tunnels—as in other cities in the Pacific Northwest that burned down and were rebuilt, including Portland and Astoria, Oregon. Beneath the original downtowns of these cities snake "Shanghai tunnels." The tunnels received their name either because they were built under Chinatowns by Chinese workers or because Shanghai was the destination for many kidnapped sailors. Countless men were kidnapped (or "crimped") to serve unwillingly aboard ships. (The word *crimp* has two potential origins: the first is a British slang word for "agent" and refers to a tactic used by the Royal Navy during the Revolutionary War and after to impress or force sailors into serving aboard ships. The other is the Dutch word *krimp*, meaning a holding tank for live fish.) These tunnels ran from downtown bars and hotels, where men were drugged or knocked unconscious, to the waterfront, where they were brought to serve unwillingly on ships in need of crews. Interestingly but inexplicably, shanghaiing was legal in the United States until Congress passed the 1915 Seamen's Act (during the early part of World War I). Women were likewise kidnapped, led to underground brothels and forced into prostitution or slavery. The tunnels were also said to hold opium dens, gambling houses and prisons. The 2020 Travel Channel program *Portals to Hell* explored the tunnels, which now play host to numerous ghost tours (I've been on several and, each time, find them fascinating, scary and unsettling), as they are said to be haunted. Unseen hands have been felt pushing and pulling on visitors and ghostly orbs (which I've seen), mist and disembodied voices and footsteps have been seen and heard.

Related to the underground, I highly recommend the 1973 ABC made-for-television horror film *The Night Strangler*, starring Darren McGavin as

Sailing ship, 1900. *Courtesy of Library of Congress, Charles E. Bolles.*

newspaper reporter Carl Kolchak. Kolchak investigates a series of murders in Seattle; the perpetrator is a ghostly, supernatural presence who hides in the underground. Although the program exaggerates the former storefronts and other pre-1889 Great Seattle Fire businesses said to still be present, it also offers a fascinating journey through the haunted Seattle underground, giving you a sense of how truly creepy the tunnels are (or are said to be).

Tales have been told for well over a century of the Shanghai tunnels being haunted by the victims of kidnappings and other nefarious activities, as well as those who perpetrated them. In their Victorian heyday in the late 1800s, waterfront neighborhoods were considered the seedier side of Pacific Northwest cities, home to saloons, brothels and boardinghouses that catered to sailors and referred to as the red-light districts and the Tenderloin. The underground continued to be used for business as well as illegal activities, including opium dens and brothels, which were reportedly present there until the 1940s, when the underground was abandoned. The underground is now used primarily for ghost tours. As you walk down Seattle's sidewalks in Pioneer Square, you can look down and see the many small, square purple (due to UV light) opaque windows embedded there in the 1890s to allow

Bound for the Klondike Gold Fields, 1898. *Courtesy of Library of Congress, Keystone View Company.*

light into the underground (very cool!). It is on the waterfront and in these tunnels that supernatural activity is said to abound. The apparitions of the undead are said to linger in these musty, wet, abandoned underground locations. Seattle has more than its fair share of paranormal legends.

By the 1890s, Seattle was gaining about one thousand residents every month. One event, starting in 1897, fueled this rapid growth: the Klondike Gold Rush. Seattle was given the nickname Gateway to the Gold Fields. As many as seventy thousand miners flocked to Seattle over the next several years, hoping to try their luck at striking it rich. Gold mining was a notoriously dangerous job; many of the men who came to the area looking

Painting of Seattle, Washington, 1913.
Courtesy of Library of Congress, Seattle Chamber of Commerce.

for a new life were never seen again. Some were lost to the wild conditions, the weather and the dangerous wildlife. They worked long days and cold nights in some of the country's most dangerous conditions. Others were killed by their fellow miners in an environment where greed and jealousy quickly turned some men into murderers. To this day, the spirits of the murder victims (and murderers) can still be felt in the city they came to, including the hotels they stayed in during their quest for gold. The hauntings are like those we've already discussed: full-body apparitions, disembodied voices and footsteps, orbs, mist, cold spots, temperature changes, items moving on their own, doors and windows being opened and shut (not by humans) and other evidence.

The Hotel Ändra was built in 1926 and originally called the Claremont Hotel, where Seattle's well-to-do upper class mingled with the gangsters and rumrunners of the 1920s and '30s. Guests have reported hearing unseen glass smashing, disembodied voices and jazz music being played by an unseen presence on the ninth floor, only to stop when investigated. No source for these unexplained noises and sounds has been found. Others report seeing a woman's apparition in 1930s clothing, said to be a hotel staff member who fell to her death from a hotel window, standing in front of their bed, only to quickly disappear when they awaken. Guests have also described witnessing items levitating and vanishing.

The 1902 Gessner or Georgetown Castle is a lovely Queen Anne–style building. Wealthy blackjack dealer Peter Gessner had the house built in 1902 and used it as a brothel and gambling hall. He committed suicide just a year later in 1903. Seattle newspapers reported that he was lovesick when his young wife, Lizzie, left him to be with a chicken farmer. Gessner is said to be one of the ghosts haunting the castle. Another spirit is said to be a young woman named Sara, who one story says was a disgruntled former employee of Gessner's who may have been strangled by a magician.

Another story has it that Sara was shot to death by an abusive pimp. Another ghost is named Mary, and she is known for her flowing hair, which (according to different witnesses) is either red or a darker color, wearing a white nightgown. Finally, there appears to be the spirit of an unwed mother, possibly Gessner's niece, who was said to have been locked in the castle's tower and separated from her baby. It is said a john or pimp killed the baby and buried it on the property (some say it was Gessner himself who did it). The baby's wailing can be heard nightly. Several of these ghosts have been seen through the building's windows.

The Victorian Italianate-style Cadillac Hotel was built in 1889, the first structure built after the Great Fire and the oldest in Pioneer Square. Designed by James W. Hetherington, the hotel first opened as the Elliot House and had fifty-six rooms. Later it would become the Derig Hotel, then the Star Lodge—until 1906, when it became the Cadillac Hotel. Legend has it that apparitions are active on the hotel's top floors and in its elevator, including the ghosts of loggers, fishermen and railroad and shipyard workers. At its opening, these workers paid between twenty-five to fifty cents a night for rooms. The first floor housed local businesses, including restaurants, a drugstore and others. The best-known spirits are those of a woman and her child, who have been heard crying throughout the hotel, especially at night. The story is that the woman was a single mother who was down on her luck, evicted from her home and forced to find refuge at the hotel. It is said that she lost her sanity, killed her child, then took her own life. In 1970, a fellow Seattle hotel (the Ozark) experienced a fire that killed twenty-one people and injured thirteen. The city passed the 1970 Ozark Ordinance, requiring all hotels and apartments to have fire sprinklers; the Cadillac couldn't afford this and closed as a hotel. In 2005, the building was reopened as the National Park Service's Klondike Gold Rush Historical Park.

Built in 1890, Merchant's Cafe and Saloon was designed by W.E. Boone (a descendant of frontiersman Daniel Boone) and is one of the oldest continually operating restaurants in Seattle and on the West Coast. It is a former brothel and is said to be home to several ghosts. One is a female spirit who has been seen and heard slamming doors, moving things around, turning the bathroom faucets off and on and whispering in men's ears. Two other ghosts are said to be a little girl and boy who haunt the basement. The story is that there was a fire in 1938 and these children died there. Employees report seeing small, shadowy figures lurking and playing tricks on staff.

The Harvard Exit Theater was built in 1925 and was first used as a Women's Century Club (a social club focused on women's history, the arts, education and community service). It became a movie house in 1968. It is said to be haunted by the spirit of a woman who hanged herself in the upstairs lounge. Witnesses say the ghost wears clothing from the 1920s and electronic devices malfunction in her presence. Employees, afraid of encountering the ghost, avoid going to the upstairs lounge. There is also said to be a male ghost who can be seen on the first floor. Witnesses say one half of his body is solid and the other half clear or translucent. He's known by the name Peter, wears old-style clothing and likes to play tricks. Finally, another female apparition is said to appear excited, as if waiting for someone, and wears Victorian-era clothing. She dissipates when approached.

The University Heights School was built in 1902, housed an elementary school and is said to be one of the most haunted buildings in Seattle. The story is that a teacher locked a young student, Brian, in the classroom closet due to his unruly behavior. It was a Friday, and the teacher and other students left for the weekend—forgetting Brian was in the closet. On Monday morning, the teacher opened the closet door to retrieve her supplies and found Brian dead. Since that event in the early twentieth century, Brian's ghost has been seen sitting at his desk, waiting for class to begin. He has also been seen walking through the school's halls at night or hiding in the bathroom. Witnesses say Brian's spirit has a terrifying aura, and those who have entered the closet where he died say they sense anger and sadness. Phantoms of other children have also been seen at the old school, playing in the courtyard and playground. They (unlike Brian) are said to be happy.

The Canterbury Ale House—which, in part, housed a market in the 1930s, a café in the 1960s and the Fredonia Apartments in the 1970s—is said to be home to the spirit of a man who, in 1978, was shot in the face during a bar brawl and died by the fireplace. Witnesses say they've seen the man's ghost in the mirror looking down and slowly raising his head to look directly ahead. He is said to be missing his face, which was shot off (needless to say, those who see him are scared to death). Employees report the jukebox turning itself on and off. Other people have reported the dark figure of a man who wanders the bar, only to disappear when approached. Finally, it is said there is a large pentagram drawn on the basement floor that (despite numerous efforts) cannot be removed.

Martha Washington Park, the former site of the Martha Washington School for Girls, also previously known as the Parental Home for Girls, sits on the shores of Lake Washington to the southeast of Seattle. It was founded in 1900 by Major Cicero Newell and his wife, Emma. The school was shut down in 1971, the buildings were demolished in 1989 and the site became a park. However, what otherwise should be a tranquil setting is in fact said to be a hotbed of ghosts and paranormal activity. It is said the spirits of mistreated schoolgirls; the school's groundskeeper, who in the 1950s abused schoolgirls and murdered staff members by hanging them from a tree; and Native apparitions from a disturbed burial ground all haunt the park. The story is that before the school was built, Natives resided on the land and buried their dead there. The burial ground was desecrated by the workmen who constructed the school buildings. Legend has it that angered Native spirits drove the school's caretaker insane, driving him to drink, abuse schoolgirls and murder staff. Furthermore, legend says that staff and students committed suicide, the dead were dumped in the well and lake and satanists held rituals on the grounds in the 1970s. Ghosts have made their presence known through disembodied sobbing and footsteps, floating orbs, showing up in photographs, placing hands on visitors' shoulders and pushing. Even a young girl's transparent, full-body apparition, wearing a nightgown, has appeared.

The Haunted Moore Theater is Seattle's oldest entertainment and performing arts venue. It was designed by E.W. Houghton and built in 1907. The foyer cost just over $30,000 in 1907 (valued at over $800,000 today) and was built with marble and Mexican onyx, solid brass fixtures and Greek statues. Being able to accommodate almost 2,500 people, at the time of its opening, the Moore was the third-largest theater in the United States. Legend says the theater once hosted a séance and was the site of Kurt Cobain's (of the rock group Nirvana) deadly overdose. It is said that the spirits are most active in the basement and make their presence known through electronic voice phenomena. Real estate developer James A. Moore is said to be one of the spirits present, in addition to several actresses including Sarah Bernhardt, Marie Dressler and members of the Barrymore acting family. Staff and visitors have reported the sounds of heavy breathing and disembodied footsteps following them.

The grand and luxurious nine-story Beaux Arts–style (with classic Greek and Roman decorative elements) Arctic Club building was built in 1916. Thousands of Klondike gold miners belonged to the club starting in 1898, with their building completed later. The club was dissolved in 1970. The building—on the National Register of Historic Places since 1978—was acquired by Hilton Hotels and Resorts, becoming part of its DoubleTree chain of hotels. The original building was decorated with stuffed polar bears and terra-cotta walruses. In addition to luxurious hotel rooms, the club housed a cigar store, a library, a bowling alley, a barbershop, a rooftop

Arctic Building, Seattle, Washington, 2009. *Courtesy of Library of Congress, Carol M. Highsmith.*

garden, a tearoom, card and billiard rooms, private dining rooms and offices for political figures to meet. It's reputed to be one of Seattle's most haunted locations: ghosts are said to haunt the third and fourth floors, with visitors reporting a phantom whistling sound. Legend has it that ghostly whispers about the gold rush, land deals and other topics reverberate around the building. Disembodied footsteps have been heard and wafting cigar smoke smelled—despite no smoking allowed in the building—and ghostly orbs seen. One specific ghostly presence is said to be that of Washington's first elected Democratic congressman, Marion Zioncheck. The story goes that he once escaped a mental institution and sent President Franklin Delano Roosevelt empty beer bottles and mothballs as gifts. He was also arrested on the White House lawn, for drunken horseplay. In 1936, Zioncheck ran for reelection and, for unknown reasons, threw himself out of his fifth-floor office window. He landed in front of his wife, Rubye Louise Zioncheck, who had just pulled up in a car in front of the hotel. Witnesses say that the building's elevator takes itself to the fifth floor without anyone pressing any buttons. Also, passersby have reported seeing Zioncheck's apparition lying on the sidewalk and even in free fall from the fifth floor.

Seattle has more than its fair share of reportedly haunted locations!

CHAPTER 10

COMMUNITIES NEAR SEATTLE

A s Seattle is a waterfront city, its neighboring communities are either on or close to Puget Sound. Although much smaller than Seattle, these towns have unique personalities—and reported hauntings of their own.

Bainbridge Island (a lovely small city on an island in Puget Sound), a thirty-five-minute ferry ride across Puget Sound from Seattle (a ride I've enjoyed several times!), has a population of twenty-four thousand. The Coastal Salish Suquamish Natives were some of the first people to live on the island and were there in 1792 when British explorer George Vancouver arrived. Chief Kitsap signed a treaty in 1855 granting the land to the United States and moved the Natives northward. The Madison Diner, a Bainbridge Island institution, was originally built in 1948 and located in Willow Grove, Pennsylvania. Owner Al Packard had it meticulously disassembled, numbered piece by piece and relocated to its current island location in 1996. It serves classic, home-cooked dishes honoring traditional American diners. The diner is said to be haunted by a playful spirit named Harry (possibly the original owner). He makes his presence known by moving items and making disembodied noises.

BREMERTON

Bremerton is directly across Puget Sound from Seattle, fifteen miles and sixty minutes by ferry but a circuitous sixty-five-mile drive away. It was founded in 1891 and had a population of 41,405 in 2019. It has been the site of U.S. Navy operations since 1891, when the first Naval Station Puget Sound was established. In 1900, the naval station became a shipyard; it was the only ship repair facility on the West Coast until 1941. During World War II, Bremerton's population rose to about 80,000, based on the large workforce required to build and maintain ships. Presidents Franklin D. Roosevelt and Harry S. Truman both visited the area during the war. It currently has several U.S. Navy facilities, including the Puget Sound Naval Shipyard and the Bremerton Annex of Naval Base Kitsap.

Bremerton Theater (also called the Bremerton Community Theatre) is said to be highly haunted. Unexplainable noises, orbs, ghostly responses to questions captured on ghost-hunting equipment, movement when no one else is present, doors opening and closing on their own, lights turning on and off on their own and strange electrical disturbances have been reported. Several ghost-investigating groups have visited the theater and reported it is haunted. One of the most haunted sites in the theater is said to be the costume loft and the "military room" in particular, full of old military jackets and helmets. One ghost, nicknamed Captain John, is said to be attached to one of the military uniforms and gets upset if items are moved. One staff member reported that when she brought a black costume hat home to repair, pictures on her walls inexplicably fell on their own. Finally, she took the hat back to the theater. Another staff member reported seeing a pair of green mechanic's pants walking on their own across the stage, and apparitions in the form of gray masses sitting on a table, seemingly talking, only to disappear. Others have reported a full-body apparition and the shadow of a man in an old-fashioned top hat and cape walking down the stairs. As with

Puget Sound Navy Yard, Pacific Squadron, 1908. *Courtesy of Library of Congress, Romans Photography.*

other theaters, ghosts are said to be attracted to the theater by old, donated items as well as the emotional energy experienced in the theater.

The Frank Chopp Apartments were first used as the City General Hospital in 1918 (at the height of the Spanish influenza pandemic). The building was later turned into the Harrison Memorial Hospital in 1942 and later still into a nursing home. No doubt many patients and residents passed away there, and there are stories of ghosts haunting the grounds. Residents report hearing disembodied voices and footsteps, unseen children laughing and running down the halls, seeing flickering lights turning on and off on their own, a full-body female apparition dressed as a nurse that walked through walls and other strange occurrences.

Bremerton's Holland Road (referred to by locals as Ghost Road) is said to be haunted by the ghost of an elderly man who, as the story goes, was hit by a car driven by a drunken teenager late at night while he was retrieving mail from his mailbox. Another ghost haunting the road is said to be that of a young girl who was killed by a drunk driver while she was riding a horse. The drunk man is said to have buried the young girl (with help from friends he called) and left the crime scene. After denying striking and killing the girl, the man mysteriously died. Years later, after the young girl's parents had died and their house had been sold, an elderly lady living at the house reported nightly hauntings. After this woman died, the house was demolished, but the hauntings are said to remain. People have reported strange, shadowy shapes moving around on the road, while others claim to have seen the full-body apparition of the girl, with long black hair, riding a horse. These sightings seem to be more frequent on foggy nights. Some drivers travel the road at night in hopes of seeing the strange shadows and spirits, but of course this is not recommended.

The USS *Turner Joy* (DD-951), a Forrest Sherman–class destroyer, is docked in Bremerton and now serves as a museum. It was commissioned in 1959 and retired in 1982, after seeing duty in the Vietnam War. Visitors and staff report the ghosts of three sailors who were killed in a shell explosion in Vietnam. These shadowy spirits have been seen moving about, and disembodied voices and footsteps have been heard. People have reported feeling a strange presence watching them as they tour the ship. Cold spots have been experienced throughout the ship, and visitors' hair regularly stands on end in fright. One male seaman's spirit is said to have an affinity for female visitors and has been seen near the lockers in the enlisted men's sleeping quarters. He's been known to startle female visitors, making his presence known. During one ghost investigation, an investigator sensed an

Inside the USS *Turner Joy*, 1968. *Courtesy of Library of Congress, U.S. Navy.*

invisible presence following her through the ship. The investigators also reported examining the refrigerator where the remains of the sailors killed in the shell explosion were kept. They reported that their fully charged camera batteries were suddenly drained with no explanation, as if depleted by an unseen force possibly trying to draw energy from them.

Des Moines is sixteen miles south of Seattle and has a population of 32,888 (as of 2020). Natives, including the Duwamish and Muckleshoot, had fished and clammed in the area for thousands of years. The city was founded in 1889 and named for Des Moines, Iowa, as several early settlers were from there. Located on the eastern shore of Puget Sound, it's nicknamed the Boating Capital of the Pacific Northwest. The ghost of a little girl named Diana is said to walk the Des Moines Beach Park each year on January 8. Ghost investigators, examining the area, report that their camera shut off on its own. A psychic participating in the investigation reported a ghostly young girl walking up a trail and other children's spirits warning the investigators to stay away from the "crabby old man." In 1917, the park was home to a children's orphanage run by a Mr. Draper. It's not clear why the children's ghosts haunt, but it appears something traumatic occurred here.

Edmonds in Snohomish County has a population of 42,853 (as of 2020). It was established in 1876 by loggers and is seventeen miles north of Seattle. It is the home of the majestic 1906 Old Edmonds Opera House. In addition to staging shows, the building has served as a skating rink and is currently home to the Edmonds Masonic Lodge. Ghosts have been reported in the building's attic, basement and elsewhere. Ghost hunters have visited and had their electronic devices light up, detecting paranormal electrical impulses. Orbs have been seen, and costumes have been moved by an unseen force.

Purportedly, a woman fell down the stairs, and although she was unhurt, it appears something unseen pushed her.

Kent (originally called Titusville but renamed after a county in England) is a large city in King County, with a population of 136,588 (2020). It was first settled by White settlers in the 1850s and is about twenty miles south of Seattle. The historic old train station built in 1927 is falling apart, well past its prime. It served the railroad industry until the 1950s, primarily the Burlington Northern Railroad (later BNSF Railway). Kent is now served by a more modern rail facility that went into operation in 2001. There have been discussions about turning the old station into a train museum, coffee shop, restaurant, visitor's center or some other retail spot, but nothing has happened to date. Those around the train station report seeing a ghost train heading straight at them, appearing at random times of night only to vanish suddenly and then reappear on the other side of the train crossing. It's interesting that we've talked about several conveyances said to be controlled by or tied to the dead; this is the second train in this book, the first being the Tacoma streetcar mentioned earlier, and we've also discussed the ghost ship of the doomed *Andelana*. Again, ghost trains, ships and other inanimate objects are said to be controlled by the undead who, in life, were involved in accidents or wrecks or suffered other sudden, unexpected ends. Also in Kent, the Greater Kent Historical Society's Bereiter House is said to be haunted. The historic house was built in 1907 for the town's mayor and his wife. It was leased to the historical society in 1996. Staff and visitors have reported objects being moved by an invisible force, cold spots, disembodied ghostly voices and the unexplained sounds of bells ringing.

Port Orchard is a city in and the county seat of Kitsap County, with a population of 14,597 (2019). In 1854, it was originally settled and a sawmill was built. It is directly across Puget Sound from Seattle (but a circuitous sixty-mile car drive). In 2015, a man reported driving his SUV into the nearby forest to take photographs of the sunset. At around five o'clock, he parked his car and fiddled with his camera for about five minutes. He then put his vehicle in reverse and looked up and into his rear-view mirror. Sitting in the back seat, he said, was a young girl with dark brown hair and even darker marble-like eyes, staring expressionlessly back at him. He stared at the young girl in the mirror without blinking for several seconds, afraid to turn his head to look behind him. He turned off the vehicle's motor, yanked the keys out of the ignition and jumped out of the vehicle. All he could say to himself was, "Oh my God! Oh my God! Are you serious? No way, no way, nope!" He gathered his courage and looked into the SUV—and saw nothing. The little girl, or whatever it was, was gone. He looked into and around the vehicle from every angle and saw nothing. After several moments, sure nothing was in the SUV, he got back in. He kept checking the mirror and spun his head around to look in the back seat several times but saw nothing out of the ordinary. He was sure of what he saw, but whatever it was had disappeared. He nervously attempted to take the photos he had gone there to take. The man had never before believed in ghosts, but this experience changed that.

Seattle's suburbs are scary (in the haunted sense)!

CHAPTER 11

EVERETT AND SURROUNDING AREA

A t the mouth of the Snohomish River, on Port Gardner Bay and twenty-five miles north of Seattle, lies the city of Everett. It is the seventh-largest city in Washington, with over 110,000 residents. The area was originally home to the Snohomish Native people, who had a fortified winter village in the area called Hilbub. British explorer George Vancouver landed in the area in 1792 and claimed the Port Gardener peninsula for England. The Treaty of Port Elliot was signed in 1855, and the Snohomish relinquished their land to the newly created Washington Territory. Settlers arrived in the 1860s to homestead and log. Everett was named for the son of investor Charles L. Colby, Everett Colby, and was incorporated in 1893 after the Great Northern Railway arrived. It became the county seat of Snohomish County (population 862,343 as of 2023) and a major industrial city, with several large sawmills. The city's economy transitioned from lumber to aerospace in 1967, with Boeing's construction of its aircraft assembly plant at Paine Field. Boeing remains the city's largest employer.

The Catholic Community Services building in downtown Everett is said to be haunted. Legend has it that a ghost named Jerri, a former social worker and manager, has been seen nervously searching for cigarettes in her translucent pocket. When a night watchman brought his dog in with him for company one night, he said, the dog began barking and running back and forth in fear. It became very cold. The man picked up his dog and immediately exited the building. It is thought that Jerri can't leave her work from her former life behind.

Everett Colby, 1910.
Courtesy of Library of Congress, Bain News.

The YMCA building on the corner of California and Rockefeller experienced a fire in the 1920s that destroyed part of the building. The building's janitor, named George, was a hero, helping several children escape the fire, but unfortunately, he died in the flames and smoke. Witnesses have said they can hear George's voice over the intercom. Also, it is said he moves exercise items in the gym. Disembodied and unexplained noises are also heard in the building. Ghost hunters have searched for George but so far have been unsuccessful in finding him.

Everett High School was built in 1880. There are reports that the school's auditorium is haunted by the spirit of a maintenance worker who, while renovating the auditorium, was killed. The man's full-body apparition has been reported by teachers and students. The spirit is referred to as the Blue Ghost. Witnesses also report seeing glowing orbs, hearing disembodied voices and footsteps and sensing other evidence of a paranormal presence.

The Historic Everett Theatre first opened in November 1901 as the Everett Opera House. It is said to have played host to such historic entertainment luminaries as the Marx Brothers, "Fatty" Arbuckle and George Cohan. There are several ghosts reportedly haunting the theater. One reported spirit is a male with a big, bushy moustache whom staff and visitors have nicknamed Smiling Al, as his face seems to remain fixed in a grin that is described as disturbing. Also, doors open and close on their own, and lights turn themselves on and off. Reports of paranormal activity increased with renovations conducted in 1993. Workers reported feeling watched. One staff member heading out of the projection room reported he couldn't close the door. The greater the force he applied, the greater the resistance he met. Suddenly, the door flew open, hitting the worker in the chest and knocking him to the floor. Another employee saw a sweater (without anyone living wearing it) lift off the floor in the projection room, float in midair, then fall to the floor. A third employee described feeling being watched, looking up from the film projector and seeing the top half of a man looking at him through the window, only to disappear.

Schooner, 1890. *Courtesy of Library of Congress, Jackson & Shark Co.*

The historic schooner *Equator* is stored in Everett and is said to be haunted. The pygmy (small, two-masted) schooner was built in San Francisco in 1888. In 1889, Robert Louis Stevenson, author of *Treasure Island* and *The Strange Case of Dr. Jekyll and Mr. Hyde*, chartered the vessel to sail from Honolulu, Hawaii, to the Gilbert Islands (a chain of sixteen atolls and coral islands in the Pacific Ocean, halfway between Papua New Guinea and Hawaii). In the 1890s, the ship was fitted with a steam engine and worked in Alaska as a tender supporting salmon cannery operations. It also served as a survey vessel and tugboat until 1956. Efforts to restore the *Equator* failed, and it was moved in 1980 to the Port of Everett, where it was enclosed in a shelter to avoid further decay. Witnesses reported "dancing lights" above the ship's hull at night. A psychic reported that these lights were the ghosts of Robert Louis Stevenson and his friend King Kalākaua of Hawaii.

On November 5, 1916, a bloody battle took place between organized labor (the Industrial Workers of the World or IWW, nicknamed the Wobblies) and local sheriff's deputies. I recall studying the radical Wobblies while I was in law school; their methods to gain better pay and working conditions (noble goals) were thought of as extreme. In what came to be known as the Everett Massacre and Bloody Sunday, between five and twelve Wobblies and two deputies were killed, with additional individuals wounded. There had been tension between Everett business owners and labor representatives due to the depressed business environment and the unions' desire for greater rights and higher wages for workers. Labor held rallies, opposed by local law enforcement, which took the business owners' side. On May 1, 1916, the Everett Shingle Weavers Union (employees creating wooden roofing shingles) went on strike. The Wobblies, a self-described "radical" labor organization, got involved. The Wobblies' representatives were beaten and chased out of town but returned with a force of three hundred onboard two vessels, the *Verona* and the *Calista*. Sheriff Donald McRea and two hundred armed "citizen deputies" met them at the Everett dock. A raging gun battle took place; no one was sure who fired first. It was said some died from gunshot wounds, while others fell overboard and were drowned. Seventy-four of the Wobblies were charged with conspiracy to murder the deputies. A trial took place, and the first Wobblie charged was found not guilty by a Seattle jury. It seemed the deputies were most likely killed by friendly fire from other deputies. The other Wobblies were released. Legend has it that the ghosts of the dead Wobblies and deputies have haunted the dock and surrounding area since.

Labor strike, 1912. *Courtesy of Library of Congress, Bain News.*

The Rucker family, consisting of matriarch Jane Morris Rucker and her two sons, Wyatt and Bethel, gained their fortune in the late 1800s by helping to establish the city of Everett and building the local real estate and lumber industry. They resided in what is called Rucker Mansion. The four story, six-bedroom, six-bathroom house with a library, a ballroom, a billiards room, two kitchens and a conservatory was built as a wedding gift from Bethel to his bride, Ruby, at a cost of $400,000 (equivalent to $11 million today). Jane is believed to haunt the home, having leaped from her bedroom window in 1907, committing suicide. Jane's apparition is said to appear at night, playing the grand piano. She is said to be particularly active during Halloween. Her apparition has been seen floating through the house, particularly her old bedroom, wearing her dressing gown (like a bathrobe). She has also been seen staring out her bedroom window, from which she jumped. The house also experiences dramatic drops in temperature, and unseen hands have touched guests. The ghost of Bethel's bride, Ruby, may also remain in the house. The mansion was named a National Historic Landmark in 1975 and was sold in 2020 for $3.5 million.

Marysville is five and a half miles north of Everett. According to stories dating back many years, the Fire Trail Road, once known as the Marysville-Pilchuck Road, is haunted by the ghost of a young man who drowned after his car wrecked and fell into a swamp. It is said he was driving too fast for the twisting road and now tries to warn other motorists of the dangerous curves. Other spirits, seen walking along the road after dark, are said to be Native men and women. One of these Native spirits is thought to be an old Tulalip chief who was murdered on what would become the road and is now searching for his killers. Mysterious glowing lights have also been seen emanating from the adjoining woods.

It's surprising how many haunted tales exist in and around Everett!

CHAPTER 12

PORT GAMBLE, WHIDBEY ISLAND AND OTHER TOWNS

PORT GAMBLE

In its heyday, Port Gamble, on the northwestern shore of the Kitsap Peninsula on the shores of the scenic Hood Canal, had one of the world's largest continuously operating sawmills and the United States' oldest—it started operation in 1853 and was shut down in 1995. The canal fjord was formed about thirteen thousand years ago when the Cordilleran ice sheet retreated. The Native Skokomish had lived here for as long as anyone could remember until 1855, when they signed the Treaty of Point No Point. William Talbot and Andrew Pope were two of the earliest White settlers when the town was founded in 1853. The area is home to whales, waterfowl, salmon, seals and world-renowned shellfish. Today, Port Gamble's population stands at under one thousand. Several town buildings are preserved as part of a historic site—a town frozen in time.

The Victorian Walker-Ames House was built in 1889 by William Walker, the sawmill's master mechanic. It sits on the hill looming over the old timber milling town and is said to be Washington's most haunted house (it, of course, has regular ghost tours). It was once the most expensive house in town but has been empty (at least of living occupants) since the mill shut down in 1995. There is a sign out front that explains master mechanic William Walker lived at the house with his wife, Emma, his daughter Maude and his son-in-law Edwin Ames. The house was near the mill in case Walker

Walker-Ames house, Port Gamble, Washington, 1968. *Courtesy of Library of Congress, Historic American Engineering Record.*

was needed for emergencies. Ames was the resident manager of the mill from 1883 to 1914 and then general manager until 1931. The house faces the waterfront as if to still welcome ships and captains. It has attracted paranormal investigators from around the world with its reported full-body apparitions, disembodied voices, footsteps on the second floor while no one living is present, wet footprints, impressions left on an old chair, cold spots and unexplained temperature changes, windows opening and closing on their own, female visitors having their hair pulled, jackets being tugged, odd smells and ghostly images in photographs. There are said to be young spirits at play, with a girl named Annabelle the most active. Periodically, someone reports seeing a figure in the attic window, even though the house is empty and locked up. One ghost is said to be that of the nanny, who is seen standing, expressionless, before disappearing.

Staff and visitors to the historic Port Gamble Theater, still in use today, have reported paranormal activity. The theater was constructed in 1906, and it played host to vaudeville programs through the 1930s. Today, the Edwardian-era Port Gamble Community Theater group makes its home here and puts on shows in the theater. One ghostly story about the theater is that during an intermission, a woman tired of waiting in the long ladies' room line yelled into the men's room, "Is there anyone in here?" A voice responded, "No, it's all free, come on in"—but there was no one there.

Port Gamble, based on its haunted history, plays host to the annual Port Gamble Ghost Conference.

WHIDBEY ISLAND AND OTHER ISLANDS

Whidbey Island is the largest island in Island County and is the fourth-largest island in the contiguous forty-eight states. It is home to approximately seventy thousand residents. Whidbey Island lies about thirty miles north of Seattle on the northern border of Puget Sound. Despite its proximity to Seattle, it has a rural and relaxed feel. When the first Europeans arrived, the island had long been home to several Native tribes, including the Lower Skagit, Swinomish, Suquamish, Snohomish and others. Spanish explorers Manuel Quimper and Gonzalo López de Haro were the first Europeans to visit the island, in 1790, followed by British explorer George Vancouver (commanding the HMS *Discovery*) in 1792. Vancouver named the island after his ship's master, Joseph Whidbey. The first permanent White settler was Colonel Isaac N. Ebey of Ohio, in 1850. Ebey also served as the postmaster of Port Townsend, a representative in the Oregon Territory Legislative Assembly and the county's first judge. On August 11, 1857, Ebey (age thirty-nine) was murdered, beheaded by Natives in retaliation for the killing of a Native chief and twenty-seven others.

The population of Coupeville, on Whidbey Island, is 1,831 (as of 2010). It is a historic district within Ebey's Landing National Historic Reserve, laid out in the 1850s and incorporated in 1910. It is also the site of several purportedly haunted locations. The Captain Whidbey Inn dates to the early twentieth century, and it is said an older woman's spirit roams the halls. A "gray lady" spirit is said to haunt the hotel and wander the grounds. Staff and visitors also report hearing the ghostly laughter of young girls coming from one room, while in another room, an unseen presence lies in and makes an impression in the bed. There is also a seemingly haunted cabin on the inn's grounds, in which disembodied voices, footsteps and electrical disturbances occur. The U.S. military's Fort Casey, in Coupeville, was constructed in 1897 and was in operation until the mid-1940s. Today it is a state park with camping, boating, hiking, historic officer's quarters, lighthouses and dark, catacomb-like, echo-filled underground passageways and bunkers. Various paranormal phenomena have been reported at Fort Casey including unexplained scratching sounds, apparitions that appear and disappear quickly, a disembodied woman's voice and screaming. Along with Fort Casey, Forts Worden in Port Townsend and Flagler on Marrowstone Island constitute the "triangle of fire" protecting the nautical entrance to Puget Sound from a hostile fleet. The old, abandoned buildings and tunnels have been described as creepy and haunted by soldiers who formerly served there. Interestingly, I wrote about another set of three military forts termed the "triangle of fire" in *Haunted Graveyard of the Pacific* and *Spirits Along the Columbia River*: Forts Canby, Columbia and Stevens, which protected the mouth of the Columbia River from possible attack. All three of those forts are said to be haunted as well. Each October, Coupeville—where the 1998 movie *Practical Magic* was filmed—turns into a month-long fright fest with scary scarecrows, barns and fields.

Also located on Whidbey Island is the U.S. Navy's former morgue, now part of Skagit Valley College. Translucent full-body apparitions have been reported wandering its hallways.

Separating Whidbey Island from Fidalgo Island, in the northwest part of Washington, is the Deception Pass strait. This strait connects Skagit Bay with the Strait of Juan de Fuca, which separates the United States from Canada. Deception Pass Bridge is actually a pair of bridges that cross the pass. The bridge—built in 1934, 1,487 feet long and 180 feet tall—is nicknamed the Bridge of Death for the many suicides that have taken place on the bridge (twelve in 2009 and fifteen in 2010 alone). The bridge is rumored to be haunted, possibly by the many suicide victims who ended their lives there. On a foggy day, visibility on the bridge is often zero and drivers are frightened to travel over the waters of Puget Sound. The narrow pedestrian lane perched on the edge of the bridge takes the fear factor to a new level. Deception Pass State Park, which surrounds the bridge, is home to mysterious coves and rugged cliffs.

The former navy exchange on Whidbey Island, built in 1942, is said to be haunted. I find this story particularly interesting, as my first job with the U.S. government was as the personnel manager of a navy exchange in California. There are stories of a spirit nicknamed the Lurker that dropped pennies and left popcorn strewn around the building overnight even though

Deception Pass, Washington, 1905. *Courtesy of Library of Congress.*

the building was empty and locked, there was no popcorn machine and popcorn wasn't even sold there. A janitor described how a male ghost chased him up some scaffolding only to disappear. An employee who worked in the former children's department claimed to find complete baby outfits laid out expertly and neatly on the floor when they arrived in the morning, even though no employee had been present overnight. The exchange building was originally an aircraft hangar for seaplanes, and there is a story that in the late 1940s, a member of an aircrew walked into the operating propeller of a P-3 flying boat and was killed. The man's ghost supposedly lurks around the building. Other witnesses reported seeing a rack of clothes ruffled as if someone was walking past, but no one was there. Another former employee who worked on the top floor of the exchange in the sign department said she

Walter Crockett blockhouse, Island County, Washington, 1933. *Courtesy of Library of Congress, Historic American Buildings Survey.*

was warned it was haunted by the ghost of a man killed in the construction of the facility. She and her coworkers frequently heard disembodied moans.

The Colonel Walter Crockett House was built in the 1850s and is rumored to be haunted. One of Colonel Crockett's sons, Charles Crockett, committed suicide in the home in 1893, and his blood is said to still stain the floorboards. Over the years, the home has gone through several phases, falling into disrepair until it was turned into a bed-and-breakfast in 1984. Strange sounds have been heard by guests in the room where Charles died, as well as the noise of smashing glass. A hand-shaped bloodstain has been observed on the ceiling, and visitors complain of feeling uncomfortable.

The old one-room San de Fuca schoolhouse on Whidbey Island, built in 1895, has many ghost stories attached to it. Children up to grade six attended the school until the 1930s. Observers driving by in the early morning have described seeing the apparitions of children on the doorstep or peering out the window. A woman who used to lie down on the grounds' grass to relax said she was awakened by a group of mischievous, ghostly kids yelling, "Wake up!" They quickly dissipated on her awakening, and she left in great haste.

The stately and majestic eighty-eight-room, five-floor, twenty-five-thousand-square-foot 1909 Moran Mansion at the Rosario Resort sits on eighty-two acres and was built by millionaire Robert Moran, who owned Moran Brothers Company shipbuilders during the 1896–99 Yukon gold rush. Moran also served as mayor of Seattle at age thirty-one, during the 1889 Great Fire. The company is said to have pioneered steel shipbuilding in the Pacific Northwest. The resort is located on beautiful Orcas Island, the largest of Washington's four major San Juan Islands, on Cascade Bay. The resort, nicknamed Shangri-La, is on the National Register of Historic Places. It is said to be haunted by Alice Goodfellow Rheem, nicknamed the Lady in Red. Alice was the wife (some called her "colorful and eccentric") of the resort's second owner, industrialist Donald Rheem (cofounder of Rheem Manufacturing Company). Her ghost has been seen in the mansion's former living quarters on the second floor (there are no longer guest rooms in the mansion, and the second floor has been turned into a museum) and on the third floor wearing a 1930s-style red dress. Her ghost has been described as mischievous; staff and visitors report being touched, laundry being unfolded by disembodied hands and her apparition passing quickly by. Guests also report hearing disembodied high-heeled footsteps in the hallways. Those who remember Alice in life said she was a larger-than-life figure, driving around the island in her large old car, playing poker and spreading scandalous stories and rumors.

The Orcas Hotel also has a ghost reportedly residing in it. Innkeeper Octavia van Moorhem was one of the first staff members to move into the hotel in 1904. She was said to be an excellent cook and catered to guests and travelers. After her death, guests reported hearing the disembodied footsteps of a woman in heels on the top floor—thought to be Octavia's spirit. The hotel's restaurant is called Octavia's Bistro in honor of Octavia van Moorhem.

In the Hotel de Haro in San Juan Island's Roche Harbor Resort in Friday Harbor, built in 1886, is said to reside the ghost of Adah Beeny. Beeny was governess and secretary to the McMillin family, who owned the local retail stores on which Roche Harbor was founded and relied. Employees report that the door to the storeroom opens and closes on its own, appliances turn themselves on and off and items move on their own. One woman reported her hands going numb as she entered the hotel's lobby because the hotel was "so haunted."

These island towns don't disappoint when it comes to haunted tales!

CHAPTER 13

BELLINGHAM AND SURROUNDING AREA

Bellingham's population in 2023 was 95,960, and it is the county seat of Whatcom County (population 228,831 in 2021) in northwestern Washington. It is situated eighteen miles south of the Canadian border along Bellingham Bay (named in 1792 by Captain George Vancouver for Sir William Bellingham) on the northern edge of Puget Sound. In 1852, the site that would become Bellingham was established by White settlers; a sawmill was built at the lower Whatcom Falls by Captain Henry Roeder. Coal-mining operations began in 1854, and the bay was a temporary staging area for the ill-fated Fraser River gold rush of 1857 to 1858 (which led to a war with the Natives). Four communities (Whatcom, New Whatcom, Sehome and Fairhaven) known as the Bellingham Bay Settlements were established by the 1880s. In 1904, they merged to form the present city of Bellingham. With railroad connections (the first railroad project was incorporated in 1883) and improved harbor facilities, Bellingham's timber-pulp operations, fish canneries and pleasure-boat building industries developed. Mount Baker– Snoqualmie National Forest (incorporated into the U.S. Forest Service in 1905) is near Bellingham, which is also a gateway to the San Juan Islands. The Lummi Native Reservation is five miles northwest of the city.

Bayview Cemetery is a public park in Bellingham and was founded in 1887. The cemetery has been described as creepy, and people have been warned not to walk around there at night, as it is said to be haunted. A floating full-body apparition has been reported in and around the tombstones. Monuments themselves are reportedly haunted, giving off strange noises,

Downtown Bellingham, Washington, 1933. *Courtesy of Library of Congress, Historic American Buildings Survey.*

lights, and temperature changes. One monument is nicknamed the Death Bed, and legend has it that any living person who lies on it will move closer to their own death. Another monument is called Angel Eyes, and the spirit of the body buried under the monument is said to roam the cemetery.

The Bellingham Herald Building dates to 1926 and serves as the headquarters for Bellingham's newspaper. Legend has it the building's elevator moves from floor to floor on its own power, as if controlled by an unseen presence. It is thought a former elevator operator was murdered in the building and he still maintains his post in the elevator. Employees in the building also report the feeling of being watched, even when no one else is present.

John Jenkins started the Spark Museum of Electrical Invention in 1985 (and served as its president) after a career in technology with Hewlett Packard and Microsoft. The museum began as an informal collection of radios, recordings and magazines. Disembodied footsteps and voices have been reported in the museum. Furthermore, someone or something (not a living person) is said to play musical instruments in the building.

Old courthouse, Bellingham, Washington, 1933. *Courtesy of Library of Congress, Historic American Buildings Survey.*

Mount Baker Theatre in downtown Bellingham's Art District is the largest performing arts center north of Seattle. The theater was opened in 1927 and has been described as haunted. Investigators recorded disembodied voices and unexplained noises and reported full-body apparitions, cold spots, balls of light and four separate ghosts haunting the theater. One ghost is said to be of a young woman named Judy. She seems to take a liking to male projectionists and ushers, who hear their names called from across the stage and report being touched on their backs and shoulders by unseen hands.

The Old Town Café was built in the 1890s. Staff have reported hearing disembodied piano music. Dishes and other kitchen items have been observed floating on their own. A female full-body apparition in a white old-fashioned dress has been observed on the second floor.

Near the town of Sedro-Woolley, twenty-six miles south of Bellingham, stood the Northern State Mental Hospital. The facility, opened in 1912, was one of the largest hospitals in Washington for the mentally ill. It included patient and staff housing, a lumber mill and a seven-hundred-acre farm. It also had a cemetery, in which at least 1,500 people are buried. By the 1950s, there were 2,700 patients living at Northern State. The hospital was closed in 1976, and much of the former grounds was made part of Northern

Empty rooms in a former hospital. *By robinsonk26 via Pixabay.*

State Recreation Area. An investigator visiting the cemetery reported being shoved to the ground by an unseen presence. One of the investigator's devices picked up his first and last name being called out by a disembodied voice. He said he experienced his heart racing, his chest tightening and eerie and uneasy feelings. The investigator's other equipment flashed green, yellow and red dots, indicating an energy source was present. It is thought that the restless spirits of the patients who once lived at Northern State remain there. According to my research, former mental hospitals as well as prisons and cemeteries have a great number of reported hauntings. No doubt this is due to the high emotions, trauma and other events that took place there.

Scary!

CHAPTER 14
PORT TOWNSEND AND PORT ANGELES

The final towns on our tour of the Puget Sound region are the coastal cities of Port Townsend and Port Angeles.

PORT TOWNSEND

Port Townsend on Washington's Quimper Peninsula is Jefferson County's seat (and only incorporated city). It had a population of 10,148 in 2020. It was first named Port Townshend by British captain George Vancouver in 1792, for his friend George Townshend, Marquis of Townshend. The city was Washington's first major port and a boomtown in the 1850s. It was described as rough and rowdy in the early days, with murders and mayhem occurring. Railroads reached the area in the 1870s. Port Townsend was nicknamed the City of Dreams, as people believed it would become the West Coast's largest harbor (it didn't, no doubt in part due to its relative inaccessibility and distance from major cities like Seattle). The Port Townsend Historic District is a U.S. National Historic Landmark District. It's now a lovely waterfront town with a plethora of Victorian buildings (I love the feel of the town) from the late nineteenth century (many of which survived—unlike other cities in the Pacific Northwest, which suffered fires, earthquakes and other natural and man-made disasters). It is significantly drier than the surrounding area, as it is in the rain shadow of the Olympic Mountains.

Bird's-eye view of Port Townsend, Washington Territory, 1878. *Courtesy of Library of Congress, E.S. Glover and A.L. Bancroft & Company.*

The 1899 Ann Starrett Mansion Bed and Breakfast is said to be home to several ghosts. One is described as a red-haired woman in a white gown, who has been observed floating throughout the hotel and on the main stairs. She is believed to be the spirit of Ann Starrett, for whom the building is named. Other ghosts are said to be that of George Starrett, who formerly owned the building, and the family's nanny, whom guests have seen wandering through the building wearing a black dress.

The former Holly Hill House Bed & Breakfast, built in 1872 and now a private residence, is said to be haunted by a man in old-fashioned clothing who walks up and down the staircase and inhabits a bedroom on the top floor. Staff and visitors have reported the smell of cigar smoke, although no one present is smoking. Disembodied piano music has been heard, although there is no piano present. The spirit of William Hill, for whom the building is named, has been reported in the parlor room where he passed away.

The impressive Manresa Castle was built in 1892 as the home of prominent citizens Charles (the city's first mayor) and Kate Eisenbeis. The castle was the city's largest private residence, with thirty rooms. It's now a hotel that some believe to be haunted by two ghosts. The first apparition is said to be a young woman named Kate who leapt to her death from her hotel room (306) in despair after her lover either failed to arrive and/or was killed. A staff member reported seeing his key ring floating in midair

Palace Hotel, Port Townsend, Washington, 2018. *Courtesy of Library of Congress, Carol M. Highsmith.*

in the room. The second apparition is thought to be of a monk who, legend has it, hanged himself in the tower above room 302. If you are looking for a haunted night's stay, you should pick one of those two rooms.

The beautiful Palace Hotel, built in 1889, was once a brothel (its nickname was the Palace of Sweets) before it became a historic hotel. It is believed to be haunted by as many as ten ghosts. The best-known spirit is said to be the ghost of a lady in an old-fashioned blue dress (nicknamed the Lady in Blue), who has been seen in rooms 3 and 4. When the spirit is present, there is a strong scent of perfume, and doors open and close on their own. Guests in these rooms have reported hearing moans and having their beds shaken vigorously. The "happy presence" of Captain Tibbals, the builder of the hotel and its former owner, has been reported in the building. Also, the apparition of an old woman in a black dress has been reported standing near the stove in room 3's kitchen. When she is approached, she dissipates. Staff have reported the friendly ghost of a little boy named Adam. He has been seen running and playing on the third floor before fading away. A menacing, shadowy apparition has been known to follow guests throughout the third-floor hallway. In the basement, a homeless man's spirit, wearing a plaid shirt, has been seen. In life, former owners of the hotel gave the man a room there. He is said to have haunted the building ever since he died. The ghosts of a woman and her children are said to haunt several floors; legend has it they died in a fire. The hotel keeps a ghost book where guests can record their paranormal experiences.

The Rothschild House Museum was built in 1868. Members of the wealthy Rothschild family called the manor house home until 1959. Some members of the family are thought to still reside there—but as ghosts, haunting their former home. Staff and guests have reported hearing doors slamming and feeling cold spots. A sad entity has been reported on the upper floor, believed to be a family member who committed suicide nearby.

The Monarch Hotel, formerly the Waterstreet Hotel, is said to be one of the two most ornate buildings in Port Townsend. It was built in 1889 and is in the historic H.D. Hill building. Haunted activity has been reported in the building. Male apparitions in old-fashioned top hats have been seen walking the halls at night, only to walk right through walls. Ghostly orbs have reportedly been photographed and videotaped. Staff and guests have reported hearing strange noises in the lobby at night. Three deaths are said

Fort Worden Historical State Park, Port Townsend, Washington, 1968. *Courtesy of Library of Congress, Historic American Engineering Record.*

to have taken place here, and there are reports that at least one of the dead still wanders around the building.

Port Townsend's Fort Worden opened in 1902 as part of the Triangle of Fire. The fort was stocked with guns and artillery and was once home to nearly one thousand troops and officers who were training to defend Puget Sound from foreign armies. The Fort's Building 298 used to be a military hospital and morgue, and the old bloodletting table can still be viewed there. There are stories of a ghostly woman appearing in the second-floor window of the old hospital every night at around ten thirty. The fort was decommissioned in 1953, and in 1958, the facility became a diagnostic and treatment center. What remains of the fort, now a historic state park (designated in 1973), are restored Victorian-era officers' homes and hidden gun emplacements. In 2019, *Outside* magazine named Fort Worden State Park one of the United States' most haunted campgrounds. A park employee told *Outside* they've witnessed paranormal activity. Other staff and visitors have reported seeing a former guard carrying on his duties even in death, a full-body apparition dressed in an army sergeant's uniform, ghosts and other presences. There are stories of disembodied footsteps heard walking through tunnels and bunkers under the fort at Artillery Hill. Hikers have reported hearing disembodied moans as well.

PORT ANGELES

Port Angeles is a city of 20,134 (as of 2021) and the seat of Clallam County. Spanish explorer Francisco de Eliza named the city Port of Our Lady of the Angels in 1791. The city is a major port (with ferry service from the United States across the Strait of Juan de Fuca to Victoria, British Columbia—we've taken it several times) and has served as a whaling, fishing and shipping village. By the mid-nineteenth century, the name had been shortened to its present form. After flooding in the early 1900s, the City of Port Angeles decided to raise the elevation of the downtown—on pilings, creating an underground in 1914. Port Angeles' underground is said to be haunted and hosts ghost tours. A ghost-hunting group has investigated and captured images of ghostly faces staring out of the windows of the underground.

Eighteen miles to the west of Port Angeles lies Crescent Lake. In addition to being a beautiful natural wonder, the deepwater lake (the second-deepest in Washington at 624 feet—after Lake Chelan, at almost 1,500 feet) is said

Courthouse, Port Angeles, Washington, 1909. *Courtesy of Library of Congress, P. Wischmeyer.*

to be home to the legendary Lady of the Lake. In life, the Lady was thirty-five-year-old Hallie Illingworth, and she was a waitress at the nearby Lake Crescent Lodge (built in 1915). She disappeared in the lake in 1937, and her body surfaced in 1940. Before her disappearance, legend has it she married local beer truck driver Montgomery "Monty" J. Illingworth. Soon after getting married, Hallie reportedly began arriving at work covered in bruises, with black eyes and broken teeth. Five months after the wedding, Hallie disappeared. Monty told the police Hallie had run off with an Alaskan sailor, and police closed the case. When Hallie's body surfaced in 1940, it was tied up with a rope (it was found she had been strangled), wrapped in a blanket and missing a few fingers, toes and the tip of her nose. It was said her body had the texture of soap, having gone through the process of saponification: the body's fat interacted with chemicals deep within the lake, turning her skin into a waxlike organic substance called adipocere. A local store owner confirmed Monty had borrowed the rope the night of the murder. Monty was convicted of second-degree murder and sentenced to life in prison. He was paroled in 1951 and moved to California. Hallie's ghost has been seen and heard repeatedly, haunting the lake and surrounding area. Witnesses report her full-body apparition walking the stairs of the Crescent Lodge during the morning hours. Staff report lights flickering, doors opening and closing on their own and music getting louder on its own. Hallie's spirit has also been seen drifting along the lake's shore and over the water, glowing, pale and translucent.

These are the final towns we'll visit on our journey through Puget Sound, and while the stories are intriguing, we also have fascinating Native legends to discuss.

CHAPTER 15
NATIVE LEGENDS

Natives have lived in the Puget Sound region for at least ten thousand years. They are known as Coastal Salish, with tribes including Duwamish, Nisqually, Skagit and Snoqualmie. Their territories covered most of western Washington State, from Bellingham in the north to Olympia in the south. Today, there are nine Native reservations in the Puget Sound region, including the Squaxin, Nisqually, Puyallup, Muckleshoot, Suquamish, Stillaguamish, Tulalip, Swinomish and Upper Skagit. There are three additional tribes that are recognized by the U.S. government but do not have reservations: the Snoqualmie, Samish and Skykomish. Finally, the Duwamish and Steilacoom are working for federal recognition. Collectively, these tribes are referred to as the Lushootseed peoples.

Many if not all of these tribes have legends about ghosts and other supernatural phenomena. These stories help Natives try to explain the unexplainable and deal with death, desecration of burial grounds and loss of lands and ways of life related to White settlers and the U.S. government. Up to 90 percent of Pacific Natives were killed by the diseases White settlers brought with them, primarily in the eighteenth and nineteenth centuries, including smallpox and measles. Wars, including the 1855–56 Puget Sound War between the U.S. military, local militias and the Nisqually, Muckleshoot, Puyallup and Klickitat tribes, with an indeterminate number killed, further negatively impacted Natives. Subsequently, treaties between the U.S. government and the Natives took lands away and forced Natives onto crowded reservations.

Pacific Northwest Native baskets and wooden figures, 1901. *Courtesy of Library of Congress.*

According to Native folklore, and Puget Sound's Snohomish people in particular, the godly figure Dohkwibuhch was their creator deity. Legend has it he began the creation of the world in the East, giving a new language to each group he created. When he reached the Puget Sound, he liked the area so much he decided to stop there.

As mentioned, first the Spanish and then British explorer George Vancouver, in 1792, arrived in the Puget Sound region looking for the imaginary Northwest passage that they hoped would provide a waterway across the continent. Fur traders followed this initial exploration, then settlers and those in search of gold. The incursions of these people disrupted Natives' lives. Even with treaties in place and Natives' reduced lands designated, White gold miners and others went wherever the riches were thought to be—including onto Native lands.

Native tribes have had differing ideas about their dead and burial. Some tribes would bury their dead in caves and ravines, walled in with rocks; some

Native petroglyph. *By Norm Bosworth 1843 via Pixabay.*

in trees; and some in or on the ground. Many times, bodies were tightly wrapped in blankets and shawls.

To the Coastal Salish of Puget Sound, community extended beyond physical life, with ongoing relationships with their deceased's souls. They believed in "feeding the dead," in which ritualistic plates of food were placed on outdoor fires. Grave houses were built aboveground, close to the villages, with carved figures and poles placed in front. The Coastal Salish believed that when Natives died, their spirits went off to a faraway country where the good things of life were more abundant—especially hunting. Personal belongings thought to be needed for the journey to the faraway land were placed alongside the dead, including weapons and pack-straps.

Other tribes, including the Chinook in Oregon and Washington (especially around the mouth of the Columbia River), have had long-standing beliefs that their burial grounds are haunted. These tribes had a strong belief in powerful spirits and a particular interest in death, specifically the fate of the soul in the world of ghosts. Many of these Natives believed that spirits coming back after death spelled doom for the living and were to be avoided. It is believed that when a person died, a malignant influence was released and able to return to earth as a ghost. These spirits haunted burial grounds and plagued the living. These Natives would take their dead far from the village, place them inside canoes, drag them ashore onto islands, hoist them up among the trees and tie the canoes to tree limbs, hanging horizontally. During the funereal process, mourners would chant a magic song to help the dead on their journey. In the treetops above the graveyard sat Kla-akhs (the Raven), watching and ensuring no one bothered the dead. Some of these Native graveyards were large, with at least forty canoes hanging in the trees. An example of Natives placing their dead far from the village in canoes and in trees involved Memaloose Island in the Columbia River Gorge, off The Dalles, separating Oregon and Washington. Lewis and Clark's Corps of Discovery sailed past the island on October 29, 1805, on their way to the Pacific Ocean. Lewis and Clark described the island in their diary as Sepulcher Island, meaning "burial island."

Desecrating Native burial grounds has preceded numerous reported instances of hauntings. In the United States, the eighteenth-century revolutionary poet, captain and newspaper editor Philip Morin Freneau believed these locations were mystical, sacred and filled with spirits that were still hunting, feasting and playing. In 1787, Freneau wrote a poem titled "The Indian Burying Ground," in which he described dead Natives

Pike Place Market, Seattle, Washington, 2009. *Courtesy of Library of Congress, Carol M. Highsmith.*

sitting and moving about the burial ground and warning strangers to stay away and not desecrate the land in some way. Unfortunately, as mentioned, White settlers, explorers and the government for the most part didn't heed these warnings.

One legend has it that Seattle's Pike Place Market is built on top of a Native burial ground. On August 17, 1907, the market officially and quickly became one of Seattle's major shopping locations for tourists and locals. It's estimated the market attracted three hundred thousand visitors per month as of 1909. Today, the market is the most popular tourist destination in Seattle (and is one of the most popular in the world) with an estimated ten million visitors per year. In addition to the diverse and fascinating vendor stalls, markets and restaurants, the market (given its age) has a somewhat creepy (to me) vibe. Numerous ghosts have been reported in and around the market. One such story involves the daughter of Chief Seattle (for whom Seattle is named), Princess Angeline—or, in her Native language, Kikisoblue. Her spirit has been repeatedly seen walking around and through the market, small in stature and wearing the red head covering she was known for in life. It is said her ghost is protecting ancestral lands. Next time you visit Pike Place Market, watch for her (I always do)!

What a way to finish our journey!

CONCLUSION

This book focuses on the ghost stories of Washington's Puget Sound region, an inlet of the Pacific Ocean and a series of connected waterways and basins and the coastal areas that bound them. The area extends from the city of Olympia in the south to the colorfully named Deception Pass in the northern part of the Sound, with the cities of Tacoma, Seattle, Everett, Bellingham and others in between. It is the second-largest estuary in the United States, after the Chesapeake Bay on the East Coast.

From the beginning of time, people have told stories and tales of mysterious and scary experiences and events and of a life beyond this physical one. These stories are often a mix of truth, exaggeration, fear, humor and wishful thinking. The more interesting of these stories take on a life of their own, become legends and are passed from one generation to the next. The stories in this book are not mine but rather tales I discovered, researched and am chronicling that have been passed along by word of mouth and other means for decades if not centuries. Hopefully, I am shedding new light, garnering fresh insights and offering unique interpretations of these tales. I can't, in some cases, corroborate the accuracy of these stories but believe they round out the fascinating history of Puget Sound nonetheless.

As a resident of Washington—and the Puget Sound region in particular—I'm fascinated by the area's history and culture. Washington was one of the last parts of what is now the United States to be explored and settled by Europeans and White settlers, making it seem more wild than longer settled and established parts of the country. For example, some cemeteries on the

Puget Sound, Washington. *By Nature-Pix via Pixabay.*

East Coast date to the seventeenth century, while the oldest cemeteries on the West Coast are generally from the eighteenth century. There is no better way to discover the beauty and history of the area than to explore its cities, towns and waterways, their history and the folklore (including haunted tales) that have been shared in this book and exist elsewhere.

Washington is known for great hiking, boating, camping, fishing, biking, clamming, golfing, cranberry cultivation, oyster farming and tourism, while state parks with nineteenth-century military forts and national historic sites welcome history enthusiasts. Bald eagles, black bears, elk, deer and other wildlife call the area home. While Puget Sound offers breathtaking, idyllic scenery, it has also been identified as one of the most haunted places in the United States. The spirits of frontiersmen, adventurers, boatmen and early settlers seem to cling to its cities and towns (Olympia, Tacoma, Seattle and others). Other lingering spirits are said to include those of Natives whose lands were stolen and burial grounds desecrated, soldiers, murderers and murder victims.

Chilling tales of paranormal phenomena abound in this northwestern corner of the United States. The Puget Sound region is steeped in haunted history. From "possessed" parks to creepy underground tunnels to hotels with spirits as permanent guests, there are many haunted attractions to visit.

Some areas, including Seattle, have high concentrations of haunted houses, ghost tours and scary sightings. Other ghosts seem to prefer more rural places. Some ghosts go much further back. Natives have lived in the area for at least ten thousand years, according to archaeological records, and some of that history is downright eerie. Ghostly sightings regularly occur at haunted cemeteries and burial grounds across the state as well as in old forts, many hotels and other locations. There seem to be many ways to get your "chills and thrills" in the Evergreen State.

The dark skies, strong winds and heavy fog that frequent the Puget Sound region round out the atmosphere of mystery. The natural and man-made disasters that have struck the area, including earthquakes, fires, tsunamis and volcanoes, have added a sense of danger and dread. So if you see someone on land who appears out of place or a ship on the water that doesn't look quite right or hear ghostly words on the wind, check again—it might be the forlorn spirits of lost souls reaching out.

I use an evidence-based, investigatory, forensic (systematic, analytical) approach to research and analyze reported haunted tales. I pride myself on my careful research, but in researching these tales, it became clear to me that not everything in them can be proven beyond a reasonable doubt.

Thank you for joining me on this journey around Puget Sound in search of things that go bump in the night! I again strongly encourage you to explore the area and (following all applicable rules and laws and respecting privacy, hours of operation, etc.) visit the many businesses and landmarks that are open to the public that we've discussed.

BIBLIOGRAPHY

Abadesco, Enrico, and Kenten Danas. "What Were the Challenges for Wastewater in Early Seattle?" University of Washington. http://courses.washington.edu.

AccessGenealogy. "Indian Legends of the Stillaguamish." https://accessgenealogy.com/washington/indian-legends-of-the-stillaguamish.htm.

Ad-Lister. "The Most Haunted Items Ever Sold on eBay." https://www.ad-lister.co.uk.

Anderson, J. "Oregon's Haunted Spots." Travel Oregon, September 28, 2016. https://traveloregon.com/.

Ausley, C. "A Haunted Seattle: 19 of the City's Spookiest Ghost Stories." *Seattle Post-Intelligencer*, October 15, 2020.

Bloom, Laura Begley. "10 Most Haunted States in America (You Won't Believe the Scariest)." Forbes, October 26, 2020. https://www.forbes.com.

Boas, F., and H. Haeberlin. *Mythology of Puget Sound.* American Folklore Society, 1924.

Boll, Cliff, dir. *Supernatural.* Season 3, episode 6, "Red Sky at Morning." Aired November 8, 2007, on the CW.

Bossio, G. "The Magic (and History) of Rosario Resort & Spa on Orcas Island." Seattle Refined, May 21, 2019. https://seattlerefined.com.

Braden, Beth. "6 Ghosts That Lurk Around Tacoma, Washington." TravelChannel.com. https://www.travelchannel.com.

Britannica. "Ghoul." https://www.britannica.com.

———. "Puget Sound." https://www.britannica.com.

BrittanyWanderlust. "Adventures in Washington." October 22, 2022. https://www.brittanywanderlust.com.

Burkitt, J. "Spooky Business—These Shops, Theaters and Inns Are Haunted by Friendly Ghosts, and Not Just at Halloween." *Seattle Times*, October 24, 1997.

Burton, Lynsi. "Ghosts in the House—The Bremerton Community Theatre Is a Haunted Hotspot, Filled with Ghostly Visitors at Night." *Kitsap Daily News*, November 26, 2010.

Campuzano, Eder. "Oregon Ghost Stories: 31 Famous Haunted Places." OregonLive.com, October 22, 2016. https://www.oregonlive.com.

Carlton Harrel, D. "Ceremony to Mark Worst Maritime Disaster in Puget Sound History." *Seattle Post-Intelligencer*, November 15, 2006.

Cauvel, Kimberly. "Getting to Know Ghosts a Mission for Skagit Valley Group." *Spokesman-Review* (Spokane, WA), October 22, 2017.

Cedeno, Jose. "Olympia's Brotherhood Lounge Might Be Haunted: Five Star Dive Bars." King 5 News, May 2, 2018.

Center for the Study of the Pacific Northwest. "George Vancouver, A Voyage of Discovery to the North Pacific Ocean." University of Washington. https://www.washington.edu.

———. "Lesson 7: The Changing World of the Pacific Northwest Indians." University of Washington. https://www.washington.edu.

———. "Northwest Homesteader: A Curriculum Project for Washington Schools Developed by Matthew Sneddon." University of Washington. https://www.washington.edu.

Cihon, Brett. "Everyone Has a Ghost Story: A Look at Olympia's Spookiest Places." NorthwestMilitary.com, October 22, 2011. https://www.northwestmilitary.com.

Cobb, Todd. *Ghosts of Portland, Oregon.* Atglen, PA: Schiffer Publishing, 2007.

Conrad, Kristy. "The Lives (and Afterlives) of Everett's Haunted Schooner Equator." Washington Trust for Historic Preservation, October 6, 2022. https://preservewa.org.

Corrections1. "10 Most Haunted Jails and Prisons in the U.S." October 2015. https://www.corrections1.com.

Cowens, Alice. "Georgetown Castle." Atlas Obscura, July 10, 2019. https://www.atlasobscura.com.

Cryptid Wiki. "Batsquatch." https://cryptidz.fandom.com.

Curtis, Dan, dir. *The Night Strangler.* Twentieth Century Fox Studios, 1973.

Davis, J. *Haunted Tour of the Pacific Northwest.* St. Anthony, Newfoundland: Norseman Ventures, 2001.

DeMay, Daniel. "Historic Port Townsend: A Haunting View of the Seaport's Past." *Seattle Post-Intelligencer*, December 24, 2018.

Department of Corrections, Washington State. "McNeil Island History." https://www.doc.wa.gov.

Dickey, Colin. *Ghostland: An American History in Haunted Places.* New York: Viking Press, 2016.

Dobkin, Finn. "Tracing the Infamous Ted Bundy's Tacoma Roots." *The Trail* (University of Puget Sound), October 25, 2018.

Doro, B. "15 Chilling Folktales, Traditions, and Objects from Around the World." In Good Taste. https://www.invaluable.com/blog/scary-folktales.

Downer, Deborah L. *Classic American Ghost Stories: 200 Years of Ghost Lore from the Great Plains, New England, the South and the Pacific Northwest.* Atlanta, GA: August House, 1990.

Dunkelberger, Steve. "Few Relics Remain of the Andelana-Tacoma's Largest Maritime Disaster." South Sound Talk, September 3, 2017. https://www.southsoundtalk.com.

———. "Five Haunted Tales of the City of Destiny." SouthSound Talk, December 10, 2023. https://www.southsoundtalk.com.

Dwyer, Jeff. *Ghost Hunter's Guide to Portland and the Oregon Coast.* New Orleans: Pelican, 2015.

Experience Olympia & Beyond. "5 Spoooooky Facts About Boo-Coda." https://www.experienceolympia.com.

Fogt, A. "Puget Sound Stories." University of Puget Sound, October 2018.

Fox, A. "This Hotel Is the Most Haunted in America." Travel + Leisure, October 7, 2022. https://www.travelandleisure.com.

Ghost City Tours. https://ghostcitytours.com.

GhostQuest.net. "Folklore & Haunted Locations Guide: Bremerton, Washington." https://www.ghostquest.net.

———. "Folklore & Haunted Locations Guide: Everett, Washington." https://www.ghostquest.net.

Ghosts of America. https://ghostsofamerica.com.

Greenman, Margo. "Haunted Harbor: A Ghost Hunter's Guide to Haunted Places in Grays Harbor County." Grays Harbor Talk. https://www.graysharbortalk.com.

Guiley, Rosemary Ellen. "Ghost of a Suicide at Haunted North Head Lighthouse." Visionary Living, May 24, 2016. https://www.visionaryliving.com.

HauntedHouses.com. "Captain Edwin R. Rogers House." http://hauntedhouses.com.

———. "Fort Worden Guard House." https://hauntedhouses.com.

Haunted Rooms America. "The 11 Most Haunted Places in Washington State." 2022. https://www.hauntedrooms.com.

Hirschfelder, Arlene, and Paulette Molin. *The Encyclopedia of Native American Religions.* New York: Facts on File, 1992.

Historic Seattle. "Cadillac Hotel." https://historicseattle.org.

Hix, Lisa. "Could Your Stuff Be Haunted? Ghostbusting the Creepiest Antiques." Collectors Weekly, October 25, 2012. https://www.collectorsweekly.com.

Jaffe, E. "Inside a Haunted House in Port Gamble." Seattle Refined, October 30, 2015. https://seattlerefined.com.

Kashino, Marisa M. "I Spent the Night in a Haunted Asylum and I Still Can't Explain What I Saw." Washingtonian, October 25, 2018. https://www.washingtonian.com.

Kasischke, Laura. "Playground Tales: Fifteen Horror Stories My Classmates Told Me." Huffpost, April 17, 2013. https://www.huffpost.com.

Kavin, Kim. "7 Most Haunted Lighthouses in the United States." Boatsetter, October 4, 2022. https://www.boatsetter.com.

Kelly, Leslie. "Port Townsend Is Full of Ghosts, Cinematic and Otherwise." Spokesman-Review (Spokane, WA). October 7, 2022.

Kendle, Kristin. "The 9 Spookiest Ghost Towns in Washington State." TripSavvy, September 14, 2022. https://www.tripsavvy.com.

Kinner, Gabriella. The Haunted History of the South Sound, South Sound Talk, October 16, 2018. https://www.southsoundtalk.com.

Ladwig, Samantha. "The Lady of the Lake Is Still Haunting This Washington Town." Culture Trip, June 30, 2018. https://theculturetrip.com.

Langmann, Brady. "Ted Bundy Said an Entity Made Him Murder—These Ghost Hunters Went Searching for It." Esquire, October 26, 2019. https://www.esquire.com.

Long, Priscilla. "Tacoma Expels the Entire Chinese Community on November 3, 1885." HistoryLink.org, January 17, 2003. https://www.historylink.org/file/5063.

MacAvoy, J. "Superstitions and Myths of Puget Sound." The Trail (University of Puget Sound), December 13, 2013.

MacCready, Parker. "Puget Sound's Physical Environment." Encyclopedia of Puget Sound. https://www.eopugetsound.org.

Mahoney, Melissa. "You Won't Want to Visit the Notorious Bayview Cemetery in Washington Alone or After Dark." Only in Your State, October 17, 2022. https://www.onlyinyourstate.com.

Mandagies. "The 15 Most Haunted Places in Washington State." https://www.themandagies.com.

McNamara, Neal. "Visit a Park Haunted by Ghosts of Puget Sound's Past." Patch.com, October 30, 2018. https://patch.com.

Merchants Café. "The Haunting."

Mindy, Everett Public Library Staff. "Haunted History Abounds in Everett." HeraldNet, November 1, 2017. https://www.heraldnet.com.

Miranda, Gabriela. "2 in 5 Americans Believe Ghosts Are Real and 1 in 5 Say They've Seen One, Survey Says." USA Today, October 28, 2021. https://www.usatoday.com.

Monster Wiki. "Agropelter." https://monster.fandom.com.

Morton, Caitlin, and Matt Ortile. "The 32 Most Haunted Places in America." Condé Nast Traveler, October 7, 2021. https://www.cntraveler.com.

National Park Service. "Death and Danger on the Emigrant Trails." December 29, 2020. https://www.nps.gov.

Olympia Historical Society & Bigelow House Museum. "Olympia's Historic Chinese History—Railroads and Riots." 2022. https://olympiahistory.org.

———. "Percival Landing." https://olympiahistory.org.

Pacific Northwest Olympic Peninsula Community Museum. https://content.lib. washington.edu/cmpweb/index.html.

Pacific Northwest Title. "5 Haunted Places in Kitsap County." https://www. pnwtkitsap.com.

Paranormal Scientific Investigations Northwest. "November 2013—The Washington State Governor's Mansion." https://psinw.wordpress.com.

Paul, Crystal. "Welcome to 'Boo-coda,' the Tiny Washington Town That Goes Hard for Halloween." Seattle Times, October 25, 2018.

Pennington, J. "Ghosts, Spooks, Opera and Masons: The Edmonds Masonic Lodge." My Edmonds News, July 24, 2021. https://myedmondsnews.com.

Perman, Cindy. "The 10 Most Haunted Cities in America." CNBC, September 19, 2019.

Porter, Richard. "Ghosts of Everett." Live in Everett, October 27, 2022. https:// www.liveineverett.com.

"A Profile of Death and Dying in America." In Approaching Death: Improving Care at the End of Life. M.J. Field and C.K. Cassel, eds. Washington, D.C.: National Academies Press, 1997.

Reeve, Scott. "From Haunted to Scary—These Bridges Don't Disappoint." Creative Composites Group, October 30, 2018. https://www. creativecompositesgroup.com.

Saltwater People Historical Society. "Misfortune in the Mosquito Fleet." December 5, 2016. https://saltwaterpeoplehistoricalsociety.blogspot.com.

San Juan Islands Visitors Bureau. "Haunted Hotels of the San Juan Islands." https://www.visitsanjuans.com.

Scott, Douglas. "Thrifty Thurston Travels on 4 Haunted Hikes within a Short Drive from Olympia." ThurstonTalk. https://www.thurstontalk.com.

Seattle Terrors. "Harvard Exit Theater." https://seattleterrors.com.

———. "Rucker Mansion." https://seattleterrors.com.

———. "Thornewood Castle." https://seattleterrors.com.

Seattle Times. "Triangle of Fire: Three Creepy Old Washington Forts Worth the Scare." October 18, 2017.

See Scan. "Dowsing Rods: Magic, Myth, or the Mind?" https://www.seescan.com.

South Whidbey Historical Society. "M/V Calista." https://southwhidbeyhistory.org.

Stensland, Jessie. "Editor's Column: Haunted Newsroom Is a Tale Untold." *Whidbey News-Times*, April 20, 2024.

———. "Whidbey Hosts Many Haunted Spots, According to Ghost Researcher." *Whidbey News-Times*, October 30, 2004.

Teich, Isadora. "12 Creepy Stories and Legends That Prove Washington Is the Creepiest State." Ranker. September 23, 2021. https://www.ranker.com.

Thrillist. "The Creepiest Place to Visit in Every State." October 5, 2022. https://www.thrillist.com.

Thrush, Coll-Peter. "The Lushootseed Peoples of Puget Sound Country." University Libraries, University of Washington, June 28, 2023. https://content.lib.washington.edu/aipnw/thrush.html.

TierOne Travel. "Haunted Places in Washington State That You Can Visit." https://tieronetravel.com.

University of Washington. "IWW History Project." https://depts.washington.edu/iww.

———. "Pacific Northwest Reference Collection: Northwest Native Americans." https://guides.lib.uw.edu/research/pnw/reference/Native_Americans.

Vander Stoep, Isabel. "BOO-coda Is Back and More Spook-tacular Than Ever." *Chronicle* (Centralia, WA), October 1, 2021.

Washington Geological Survey. *Guide to the Mima Mounds*. https://www.dnr.wa.gov.

Washington State Parks. "Deception Pass State Park." https://parks.wa.gov.

WestsideSeattle. "Beach Park, SeaTac Hotel among Highline Haunts." October 25, 2005. https://www.westsideseattle.com.

Wick, Jessica. "Don't Drive on This Haunted Street in Washington…or You'll Regret It." Only in Your State.com, May 21, 2026. https://www.onlyinyourstate.com.

———. "Port Gamble Is Allegedly One of Washington's Most Haunted Small Towns." Only in Your State, September 20, 2022. https://www.onlyinyourstate.com.

Williams, David B. "Mosquito Fleet." HistoryLink.org, February 2, 2021.

Wood, M. "The Most Haunted Hotels in the World." USA Today, October 30, 2014.

Wynkoop, Gena. "Take a Haunted Road Trip around Western WA." Seattle Refined, October 29, 2016. https://seattlerefined.com.

Yacht Were You Thinking? An A–Z of Boat Names Good and Bad, Puget Sound Maritime. Based on Jonathan Eyers's book. January 29, 2018.

ABOUT THE AUTHOR

Courtesy of David Kitmacher.

Ira Wesley Kitmacher is a published author of books on the American Pacific Northwest (*Haunted Graveyard of the Pacific, Spirits Along the Columbia River, Haunted Puget Sound* and *Pacific Northwest Legends and Lore*), European (*Monsters and Miracles: Horror, Heroes and the Holocaust*) history and folklore and conflict resolution (*Solomon's Steps*). Also, two of his history and folklore books have been adapted for grade school readers (*The Ghostly Tales of the Pacific Northwest* and the upcoming *The Ghostly Tales of Puget Sound*).

Ira served as a professor for over a decade, teaching graduate-level courses at Georgetown University in Washington, D.C., and Portland State University in Oregon, as well as undergraduate courses at Grays Harbor College in Aberdeen, Washington; Clatsop Community College in Astoria, Oregon; and Western Nevada College in Fallon.

Ira is a retired senior U.S. government executive. He is also an attorney, consultant, cruise ship onboard historian, tour guide, commissioner on a county historic commission and member of the History Writers Association. He has been featured on television programs, documentaries, radio shows and podcasts, in newspapers and magazines, at national and regional conferences and at museum and book events. Ira holds juris doctor, master of science and bachelor of arts degrees. He is a graduate of the Harvard

Mount Baker and Deception Pass, Puget Sound, Washington. *By Ken 1843 via Pixabay.*

University John F. Kennedy School of Government's Senior Executive Fellows Program and other leadership, conflict resolution and change management programs.

Ira has a passion for history and folklore.

FREE eBOOK OFFER

Scan the QR code below, enter your e-mail address and get our original Haunted America compilation eBook delivered straight to your inbox for free.

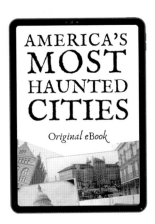

ABOUT THE BOOK

Every city, town, parish, community and school has their own paranormal history. Whether they are spirits caught in the Bardo, ancestors checking on their descendants, restless souls sending a message or simply spectral troublemakers, ghosts have been part of the human tradition from the beginning of time.

In this book, we feature a collection of stories from five of America's most haunted cities: Baltimore, Chicago, Galveston, New Orleans and Washington, D.C.

SCAN TO GET
AMERICA'S MOST HAUNTED CITIES

Having trouble scanning? Go to:
biz.arcadiapublishing.com/americas-most-haunted-cities

Visit us at
www.historypress.com